FROM START TO Six Figures

MY 12-STEP SIX-FIGURE SUCCESS SYSTEM FOR CHRISTIAN FEMALE START-UP COACHES

LATOYA EARLY

Copyright © 2021 Chase Great Enterprises

All rights reserved. No part of this publication may be reproduced, distributed, or transmitted in any form or by any means, including photocopying, recording, or other electronic or mechanical methods, without the prior written permission of the publisher, except in the case of brief quotations embodied in critical reviews and certain other noncommercial uses permitted by copyright law. For permission requests, write to the publisher, addressed Attention: Permissions Coordinator at the email address below.

Chase Great Enterprises info@ChaseGreatEnterprises.com
www.ChaseGreatEnterprises.com

Editing and Interior Formatting
House Capacity Publishing LLC
www.HouseCapacity.com

ISBN-13: 978-0-578-91105-2

A NOTE TO READERS

This publication contains the opinions and ideas of the coaches at Chase Great Enterprises. It is intended to provide helpful and informative material on the different subject matters listed. The strategies in this book may not be suitable for every individual; however, we encourage each reader to be open to a new perspective.

I am not a therapist, counselor, or medical doctor. According to the coach's code of ethics, we are encouraged to advise anyone who may be suffering from mental illness to seek medical support.

Contents

Intro	Make a Decision	7
Step 1	Accept the Challenge	13
Step 2	Submit to the Process	27
Step 3	Decide There Are No Other Options	43
Step 4	Master Your Message	51
Step 5	Solve a Problem	61
Step 6	Niche Marketing for Christian Coaches	71
Step 7	Know Your Ideal Client	89
Step 8	Tell the Story; Don't Sell the Service	99
Step 9	Create an Offer	109
Step 10	Shift Your Mindset	123
Step 11	Scale to Six Figures	139
Step 12	Start to Six Figures	153
	About the Author	167

MAKE A DECISION

Before we get started, let's make a few things clear. This is not a "get rich quick" book for coaches. This book is a power-guide to help you start, grow and monetize your coaching business from *Start to Six-Figures* in your niché. This book is designed to give you a step-by-step process on how to build your coaching business using niché marketing strategies for coaches. I will share the exact process that took my coaching business from *Start to Six-figures*. This process has taken me years to develop, but you'll be able to implement the strategies shared and see results in no time.

I know you've heard it before: marketing gurus promising you multiple six figures in your coaching business. If you practice these "three strategies" ... well, that isn't what this book is about. I want to share my process of earning my first six-figures in my coaching business and how you can do the same. I've been in the coaching industry for well over nine years at this point, and the journey taken wasn't by far the easy route. I want to share major milestones in my business that I was required to overcome to go from *Start to Six-Figures* in my coaching business. You have everything you need right in front of you. I want you to learn how to maximize what you have, reach your goals, and believe that you, too, can create a financially sustainable coaching business.

Marketing for coaches can seem nearly impossible when it seems like you're entering a saturated industry. Trust me; it only feels that way when you become consumed by what other coaches are doing and trying to compare. The coaching industry isn't oversaturated at all. It's an open industry that offers the opportunity to create your own wealth. According to census.gov, as of 2021, there are 330,094,283 people in the U.S and 7,744,298, 5342 ... 43 ... 44 worldwide. There is room for you. The art behind building a financially stable coaching business is knowing how to do it and knowing how to scale it. The number one thing that sets you apart in your coaching industry is your niché. The clearer and more confident you become, the more you stand out.

Since working with Christian female startup coaches, I've learned that it's not marketing that most coaches struggle with. There are three major areas: consistency, confidence, and clarity. We're going to get into these three major concepts later in the book, but before moving forward, I want you to make a decision. I want you to decide whether building a six-figure coaching business is what you really want. Don't wait until you read the book and decide whether the process will be easy enough for you to say yes. I want you to make a gut-wrenching decision in this very moment that going from *Start to Six-Figures* in your coaching business is your ultimate goal—by any means necessary. Why am I having you make such an important decision before you even start Step 1? Because your decision at this moment is what will determine how you process the information in this book and the outcome of your success. If your intention is to find ways to make money online and coaching seems like the way to go, then I want you to stop, close the book, and find something else to support you. If, at the bottom of your heart, you know coaching is how you will fulfill your purpose in life, then let's keep reading.

The power of your intent will either keep you stuck or catapult you into your wildest dreams. I remember starting my coaching business over nine years ago. I had no idea what a coach was outside of a sports coach. I can vividly remember the day God shared with me that my road to fulfilling His purpose in life was through Vision Coaching. I was floored. First, I had never heard of such a profession, and second, I had no idea how to bring forth the vision and reach the income I truly desired in my life. By this time, I was on business number eight, trying to figure out how to leave my footprint in the world, break generational curses, and live a life in financial freedom. I wasn't sure how to reach these life goals through coaching, but after seven unsuccessful businesses, I was willing to try.

I've gone from event planning to a small demolition company to co-owner of a semi-professional basketball team. I was so busy trying to figure out how to create a profitable business that I wasn't focusing on how to create a business that fulfilled purpose and generated profit. Now let me pause here because I want to help you recognize how powerful it is to start a coaching business and be able to generate profit. Having the ability to exchange profit for authentic, life-changing transformation shouldn't be viewed lightly. It takes a lot of mindset and lifestyle adjustments to finally get to a place where you value your value.

Throughout my journey of entrepreneurship, I've learned that there are two types of people: wealth creators and wealth generators. Wealth generators are those who can take a proven concept and multiply the profit over and over. This type of pro-creation comes after you've learned how to efficiently scale your coaching business. Now the wealth creator, that's you. The one who has taken an idea, built a business from scratch, and created wealth from it. Now, I know we can probably debate whether coaching is a business model from scratch or if it's generated based on books such as this. Keep in mind that no matter how many strategies you read or people you follow, there is a certain formula that only *you* can implement that will ensure the success you desire. Coaching is *not* a cookie-cutter industry. We all have our strategies and secrets to success, but the real secret is *you*. Your mindset is the key to whether you win or lose in this industry. Your mindset is what determines whether you become a wealth creator or a wealth generator.

When you think about what life could be like fulfilling purpose and creating profit, what do you imagine? You want to take a moment and really discover the deeper meaning behind your intentions. You want to make sure that if you're spending your time building something from idea to product to wealth, it's something that you love, brings meaning to the world, and pleases God. Coaching had become that thing for me. After examining my life's history, patterns, and characteristics, I was able to see how the gift of coaching had been in me all along— I had yet to learn how to captivate the gift and turn coaching from just a business into a full lifestyle. Over the next 12 steps, I want to help you turn coaching from just a business to a profitable, fulfilling lifestyle. The strategies that I will share are the exact strategies that took me from *Start to Six-Figures* in my coaching business.

What makes this book so powerful is your start may not be where my start was. I've been coaching for a while, but my start didn't start nine years ago. My start began the moment I decided in my heart that I, too, could have more. I, too, could generate a multiple six-figure income in my coaching business if I did just one thing—changed my mindset. Mindset is just one of the steps we will cover in this book, but it is definitely the most powerful step.

The 12 Step Six-Figure Success System is not a time-stamped formula. It's not a 12-week program; it's a formula that encourages you to examine and apply 12 proven strategies to grow your coaching business. The 12 steps I will share will require both internal and external work. I had no idea the gateway to my first six-figures wasn't connected to my skill or talent. It wasn't connected to how many clients I closed or the conversion of my sales pages, but how I viewed money and my value in coaching. Are you coaching for popularity or purpose? Are you in coaching to change the mindset of your client or the moment? Only changing the moment will keep you running in circles but learning the true art of changing the mindset will help you break free in areas of your life you would have never imagined. Now understand this and hear me good: everyone around you won't understand this journey, so be prepared. Don't enter into this assuming that family and friends will understand your journey. Know that this journey is personal, and it will require an immense amount of focus, confidence, and strategy.

So, if you're ready, access your digital workbook (you can download this workbook by visiting www.starttosixfigures.com), and let's dive into your journey of taking your coaching business from *Start to Six-figures*.

Step 1

ACCEPT THE CHALLENGE

Step 1
ACCEPT THE CHALLENGE

Have you ever been dared to do something? I mean, like called out and dared to do something that you knew in the bottom of your gut there was a possibility that you could fail? How did that make you feel? By nature, I am not a competitor. I can remember the first time I tried to compete in a sport. I was probably in grade school; to be honest, I was so humiliated and embarrassed I don't even remember how old I was. That's how far I've tried to bury this memory. At that age, I wanted to be a part of something, wanted to feel like I had something unique. Wanted to be a winner in some sort of competitive sport so that I could prove to the world that I was good at something, that I was good enough. So, I signed up for track. During this time in my life, I was battling with my identity hard. I was trying to figure out who I was, how to be me, and what that looked like exactly. I signed up for track, and let's just say, I wasn't up for this challenge.

The day of the relay had come, and although I've tried to bury this memory, I can remember it like it were yesterday. It was my first time competing, and it was my time to run. I was excited and nervous all at the same time. I thought this was my time to be good at something—this was my time to prove to myself and my parents that I did have a special talent that can be cheered on by the world. The race started. I was in position to receive the baton and take off. I thought I had it in the bag. All I remember is taking off running at full speed, one hand shaped like a blade the other with the baton... form was just right... I was determined, then it happened. I'm still embarrassed writing this 30 years later. I hit the pavement. The reddish, brownish track pavement that burned you if it got too hot on a hot summer day. The stands were filled with parents and peers, and for the first time in my life, I was publicly humiliated. I just laid there. I had decided the moment I felt myself falling that I was not getting back up. I let the fall defeat me. My parents came from the stands rushing to see if I was okay. My coach wanted to make sure I didn't hurt myself, and I'll be honest, I was more hurt from the embarrassment than the actual fall.

Yes, I did it. I faked an injury so that people would have more sympathy for me than laughs. I pretended to be hurt so that I could disappear from that place and never return. This was my first lesson of what failure truly looked like. Yeah, I know I was a kid, but instead of cowarding out after the fall, I should have gotten up and kept running—but I was too embarrassed. I had no idea that this would be my first experience of failure.

This was the first time in my life I had decided to take a risk and do something that I thought I would love, and it defeated me. What makes this story crazy is, until this day, I still love running, but I must admit that embarrassment altered my confidence. This is the one experience that stopped me from taking dares. I never wanted to experience that level of embarrassment ever again, and because of that, I never betted on myself to help win a competition in a sporting event. Now I will say this event didn't stop me from being active, but subconsciously it altered my entire life, and it kept me from sports that required all eyes on me for the win.

Having this experience not only made me shy away publicly, but it showed up in my business. I never wanted to be the center of attention in case I failed, but that was only a distraction to keep my voice silent and the vision hidden. Have you experienced some sort of embarrassment that stopped you in your business?

ACCEPTING THE CHALLENGE

There are so many coaching moments in that story, but I'm going to try and keep focused on the subject at hand. Accepting the challenge of becoming a coach used to sometimes feel like that moment when I experienced the fall. Being confident in what you can offer people but not confident enough to get up when you fall. Saying yes to your call in coaching can seem like a difficult decision, especially when you're facing a challenge where you can't see the outcome. Your subconscious tends to remind you of all the times in your life where you didn't measure up in hopes of stopping you from experiencing that same hurt again. This is why accepting the challenge is such a critical step in your business. Going from *Start to Six-figures* in your coaching business can be easy breezy, but if you're not up for the challenge and the process, you may feel yourself pulling back and creating excuses as to why this just won't work for you. Your thoughts will begin to remind you of that moment you were embarrassed. "You don't want to go back there, do you?"

Think about the many times we've justified fear by saying, "It just doesn't work for me," or "I can't do it like they do it." Success doesn't look the same across the board. We can offer strategies, support, and accountability, but the way you apply action will yield a different result. Before we get knee-deep in the strategies, I want you to define what success is for you. When you think of being a success, what do you envision? You can attain the exact things you've envisioned, but you have to be willing to stay the course.

After that awful fall in grade school, I gave myself excuses as to why I could never again compete as an individual. I had allowed the pain of failure to creep in and rob the majority of my adolescence and my adulthood, if I'm honest. While we're not talking about childhood sports, this type of experience could truly paralyze you in launching your business and creating the six-figure income you desire. This is why it's important when entering into a profession that requires lifestyle changes for others that you take a moment and examine different areas of your life that could reappear in some of the exact areas in which you're looking to support others. If you know God has called you to be a Confidence Coach, then the first step to accepting the challenge is finding areas in your life where you were challenged with confidence. Why is this important? What you hide will eventually show up in your business and in your client. Your ideal client is a reflection of who you once were, assuming you've gone through the transformation process already. Accepting the challenge requires a self-examination so that you can identify the areas your ideal client needs you most. As a coach, people recognize us as an example. An example of what life could be like on the other side of the fight. Not that your life has to be perfect, which is why I teach niché marketing for Christian female startup coaches, but that your life reflects growth, change, and transformation in the areas you're establishing your expertise.

Think about it, you're on the path of establishing yourself as an expert in confidence, and you find yourself being challenged day after day in the exact area in which you want to serve and support others. Do you think this is a coincidence? Absolutely not; it's all a part of the process. The day you accept the challenge is the day you begin the process of pruning behaviors and beliefs that will keep you from the success you desire in your coaching business. Now here's where the challenge comes in. With accepting this responsibility of changing the lives of others, there are a few hidden requirements that you want to be sure to adhere to. We see all the time coaches, influencers, teachers, and pastors telling us one thing and doing the complete opposite. Don't be that coach. Be the coach that stands with integrity and practices what she teaches. Be sure to access your digital implementation guide to support you through this exercise.

DISTRACTIONS

1. When the going gets tough, it doesn't mean you stop. I know we are naturally compelled to believe that distractions are warning signs, and to some extent, they can be. They warn you that if you choose to ignore distractions, there is greater on the other side. Distractions can be anything that causes discouragement or interruption to the process of meeting your goals and fulfilling God's purpose for your life. Notice I didn't say "avoid" distractions. You can't avoid distractions; they're inevitable. They will come, but when they do, learn how to identify them and void them out. This is a key you will need throughout your entire process, so keep it close.

Distractions can be both good or bad. Whether you've just received a promotion on your job, you have to stop and feed the kids, or you keep procrastinating on finishing that project, anything that interrupts the process is a distraction. The question is, how do you void them from your process? Visit the implementation guide and examine the distraction that has kept you stuck.

Keep in mind, distractions will come from any area. The exact area you want to serve and support your ideal client is the exact area you will see distractions. Distractions are continuous. The more focused you become in your business, the more they will surface. This is why team building will become more and more important as you grow your six-figure business. We will talk more about that later. Your distractions are not intended to be a stop sign— more so a yield sign. Observe the distraction, examine why it has surfaced, void it out and then proceed with caution.

2. The very thing you want to do in the lives of others, you first have to do in your own life. There is only one Savior, and He has already died and arisen on our behalf. Your coaching business isn't an opportunity for you to go out trying to save folks; your responsibility is to provide an alternate route to the success they desire in the area of your expertise. The most effective way to implement power strategies that are surefire to help your client transform is to take the time to apply the change to your life first. You're your first testimony. Once you're able to experience the transformation firsthand, it's easier to believe that the transformation can happen in the lives of others, and it's a much easier way to connect with your ideal client. Later we're going to discuss in detail how to clearly identify your ideal client. If you're going to teach healthy living, put the cookies down and start practicing it. Don't do a half job. Accept the challenge and fully commit. The last thing someone wants to do is invest in a half-committed coach who believes in the idea of "What happens in my home is my business." Yeah, you're right—it is your business, but the moment you accept the challenge and decide to be a successful guide in someone else's life is the

moment you forfeit what makes you comfortable and start exercising what's right.

I know you didn't think going from Start to Six-Figures would require all of this and just think: you're only in step one.

3. Accepting the challenge will require one crucial decision from you. It will require you to decide whether you will believe enough in your gift to take the risk. I learned the saying back in high school when I was in the JROTC program, "No Risk, No Reward." At the root of your risk are rewards much greater than your fears. There are so many breakthroughs and freedom buried deep in your risk. Every time you tell yourself, "Next month, in the New Year, when my money gets better, when I finish this, when my kids are done with that..." you're only giving yourself a justified excuse to procrastinate. The root of procrastination is fear. The reason you haven't accepted the challenge is not that you don't have the time or because you don't know where to start. The reason you haven't fully accepted the challenge is because you're afraid of the outcome and the responsibility. You're afraid of the "What if this doesn't work," thought, and I understand. I've been there, but I challenge you to ask yourself, "What if it *does* work?" What will you gain for trying, and what will you lose for not? At the tender age of nine, I learned

that failure isn't about falling; it's about falling and not getting up to try again.

Are you ready to accept the challenge? We define a challenge as anything that disputes the truth or validity of your coaching. Think about it; your thoughts, people around you, or maybe even family may dispute the validity of your gift and right to exchange your gift for profit—but that's what makes it a challenge. Your coaching business will require you to make some uncomfortable decisions and maybe even disassociate yourself from longtime friends. Why? Because it just may be what's challenging your truth. People or thoughts may do whatever they can to challenge the validity of your truth. Your truth is what you believe it to be. Your truth is what the Word of God says for your life. Your potential is in your perspective. Accepting the challenge will force you to push through uncomfortable situations, circumstances, and thoughts, but you can do it.

Leaving my 9-5 with three babies and a new marriage was challenging. His family thought he had made one of the biggest mistakes of his life. Sometimes I questioned whether or not they were right. Accepting the challenge made me uncomfortable. It challenged my thoughts, my marriage, and my finances, but if I aborted the vision, I would have never seen the other side. Your endurance is what builds character; it's what prepares you for the six-figure months and life-fulfilled days. I get it: this isn't everyone's journey. Some people jumped into coaching without a spot or wrinkle, but one thing I know for sure is saying yes to God will require change. Change is uncomfortable.

CHOOSE YES

Now, let me be sure to make this clear. You don't accept the challenge once; you accept the challenge daily. This is why this is the first step in my 12 step process. Every day will require a "yes" from you. Every day I wake up and decide to Chase Great. Yes, I will push through. Yes, I am a multiple six-figure earner in my business. Yes, it is challenging at times, but I've said "yes." Yes, I don't feel like it today, but I've said "yes." Yes, I am an adult, and I can do what I please, but I'm not just saying "yes" for me, I'm saying "yes" to the people I'm called to serve and support. Your journey will require you to say "yes" daily. Even when it's not making sense, or you just really don't feel like it. Every Monday, I host a free live training in my Facebook community, and there are some Mondays when I just don't feel like it. I still say "yes." Not for me, but for the people I am called to serve and impact.

Now don't get confused with the decision of "yes" and the power of "no." Something my dad used to say to me all the time was, "When you say 'yes' to one thing, you say 'no' to everything else." Your decision to say "yes" unlocks the power behind "now." Accepting the challenge requires focus and consistency. It requires boundaries and the courage to say "no" when necessary. You may not be able to show up to everything for everyone. You can't coach everyone in your family because they may think your services should be free for them. Learn the power behind your "no" the moment you decide "yes." Understand that your gift in coaching is unique, and it's valuable. You must be sure to treat it that way, or no one else will. The more confident you become in your "yes," the easier it becomes to say "no."

Here's what I mean when I say you have to accept the challenge daily. When I first said "yes," I was so excited. I was excited to share my gift with the world. I was excited to lay out in full detail how to take any business from start to success; with this approach, here's what I learned the hard way:

1) My words began to lose their value because I wasn't valuing them. I was giving it away for "free 99," but I wasn't considering the consequences.

2) Because I was saying yes to everyone, it was harder for me to establish myself as an expert with authority because there was nothing significant about my process. There were no boundaries. I didn't require an appointment to work with me. I would let anyone pick up the phone and pick my brain. Now, I'm not saying to start being cocky towards people, but I am saying establish a boundary. What separates you from a friendly conversation and a coaching conversation? How many times will you allow someone to send you a virtual invitation for coffee and conversations to pick all your value for free? Listen, these are the same experiences I had to endure and learn from.

3) Not only was it hard to establish myself as an expert, because I was so used to saying yes, when I finally said no, I felt guilty.

Does this sound familiar? Accepting the challenge will require you to release yourself from some old habits and thought processes that will keep you stuck, one of them being people-pleasing. This character flaw must be destroyed. The moment you start to feel guilty when you tell someone no as it relates to the growth and sustainability of your business is the moment you need to be free from people-pleasing and the opinions of others. How does one free thyself, you ask? Who do you need to be freed from? First, through prayer, asking God to help build your confidence and remove any doubt you have about the success of your business, and second, you need to check the root. This is an exercise I take the coaches through to help them truly identify their coaching niché. Let's get to the root of why people-pleasing is a struggle. Whose approval are you truly searching for? Why does your truth rest in the words of someone else? This is why accepting the challenge is a daily decision. There will always be something that will try to disrupt your pursuit to greater— it's up to you on how you will handle it. When you say yes to Christ and your assignment to fulfilling His purpose for your life, you have to say no to the distractions that will follow.

Step 2

SUBMIT TO THE PROCESS

Step 2
SUBMIT TO THE PROCESS

Now that you've said yes, let's discuss strategies to submit to your process and remain confident and consistent in your yes. When you think of submission, what do you think of? That word can make you feel a little uncomfortable if used in the wrong context. However, in this book, it means to totally surrender to your *Start to Six-figure* process through Christ Jesus. It's preparing for the unknown, accepting the possibilities, and breaking through what may seem impossible. This process requires a lot of renewing of the mind. Submitting to the process means that every day you say "yes," you understand distractions will come. Your patience will be tested, and your yes may sometimes waver. But you can't let the temporary experiences cause a long-term effect. In the beginning stages of my process, I thought I had given my coaching business my all. I thought I was totally submitted and prepared for what was coming, but I was wrong. I wanted success so badly I couldn't see what I needed to do internally. I was so excited about the assignment, I hadn't fully committed to the process.

Your process to six-figures will require internal work. Two major areas I had to address during my process were pride and rejection. When we imagine pride showing up in our lives, we assume arrogance or vanity, but pride can show up in many different ways and areas in your life— including your business. I can remember when pride took its place in my life. I hadn't even noticed this was the root of what I call my "independent woman" syndrome. I went through my internal process, trying to prune myself of anything that would stop me from reaching my greatest desires in business. When rejection and pride surfaced, I had no idea how to rid myself of what those experiences did to my mental health. Later in the chapter, I will take you through the exact process I took myself through once I identified rejection as one of my rooted issues.

PRIDE

Pride was a different type of healing process. I wrote in my journal asking myself the golden question, "LaToya, why do you have such a hard time asking for help?" The answer didn't come right away. After having an intense dialogue with my husband on his podcast, I learned that my issue with asking for help was rooted in an experience I remember between my parents. My mom was working two jobs and told my dad that she needed help. His exact words were, "Two jobs were for two people." This statement stayed dormant in my subconscious for a long time, hence why I felt like I never needed to ask for help. I never wanted to feel the type of rejection my mother felt at that moment. I was raised by a mother who, at a very young age, showed me what hard work looked like. If I ever wanted the "finer" things in life, it would require hard work and dedication. This is where pride found its way into my life. It wasn't until I was drowning in business before I noticed this character flaw. I noticed that I had preferred to figure things out on my own because I assumed that would make me a stronger business owner. It wasn't making me stronger, it was keeping me stuck. After learning this about myself, I made a decision. I decided that pride could no longer drive me in circles. Once I was free from pride, I sought the help I needed and truly transformed my business.

REJECTION

As a child, I felt rejected a lot. By family, friends, even my parents at times. Even as an adult, I've struggled with rejection. To truly maximize my gift, I had to get to the root of the rejection I experienced and no longer allow those memories to distract me from my pursuit. When we talk about submitting to the process, we're identifying areas in our lives that will prevent us from reaching the overall goal. Being rejected in your childhood or as an adult can really create mental barriers in your pursuit of success. It can create roadblocks of fear and procrastination without you even realizing it. The moment I started to see myself struggle in sales was when I realized that something was wrong. I had a hard time asking for the sale, being bold and confident with pitching myself to people and other businesses. I tried to blame it on being an "introvert," then I realized that was nothing but an excuse to avoid going after the sale.

One day, rejection paid me a visit, and it showed up on a call with a potential client. I was sitting in my office trying to enroll a client into my program, and it revealed itself like I had never seen before. Most times, when we think of rejection, we think it only appears in relationships. On this particular day, I learned that relationships, in most cases, are where it starts. However, rejection appears in any area that can recreate that emotion you had the first time you were rejected. Think about it, whether rejection started for you in the womb, from a parent or a school peer, it was rooted in the dismissal of a relationship. Rejection showed up in my lack of confidence and inability to enroll a client into my program. Yes, It's really that deep. Your subconscious stores emotions that are connected to you not being accepted by someone. The moment you enter a situation where someone can tell you "No," deny your service, ignore you, or give you criticism, your mind automatically reminds you of that emotion which causes you to withdraw. Later in the book, we're going to talk about not being afraid to ask for the sale at the price point you desire. However, to reach that breakthrough moment, we have to identify what's keeping us stuck.

Use this time to examine your process, examine areas in your life, and current ways of thinking that could be holding you back. Are you truly submitted to the process, or are there mental and emotional roadblocks keeping you stuck? This self-examining process will free you from mental blocks that have talked you out of going after what you truly desire in your coaching business. You've been told you can achieve the impossible, but do you really believe it? If rejection is one of the strongholds in your life and business, then we need to address it. I want to use this time to take you through my rejection recovery exercise, which I have used with dozen of coaches. The goal is to help you identify where rejection started and how it's showing up in your businesses without making a decibel of noise. Here's a hint: it's louder than you think.

I want to take you through a series of exercises, and I want you to be honest and free with yourself. This is the perfect time for self-examination so that we can really understand and remove the root of this distraction. Make sure you have your digital workbook for this exercise so that you can walk yourself step-by-step through the process. Your brain has created a response to every situation that reminds you of an experience: when someone told you "No," an idea that was refused or dismissed, or you felt completely rejected by someone. Your emotions then respond to that experience in the present and create a presumed result, now preventing you from ever seeking elevation or success outside of your comfort zone.

1. Pray.

We need the Holy Spirit to reveal to you areas in your life where you've experienced rejection. I encourage you to pray before we enter this exercise because we tend to remember what we want and bury what hurts, creating more damage later.

2. Identify the problems in your life that are the result of the rejection.

Even if you're unsure, write it. The fact that you had to ask yourself shows that it's connected. Here are a few signs that rejection may be holding you hostage: being insecure, having a hard time growing successful relationships, lack of trust in people, being extremely sensitive to other people's opinions, not saying "no," being a bully, being mean to others.... the list can go on. For the sake of this lesson, rejection in one area can show up in your business and prevent you from creating relationships and making money.

3. Sacrifice time over the next 30 days and pray daily.

This process is not just a "one and done." This process will bring up old feelings and emotions you thought were gone, but come to find out, they've been hidden so deep and for so long that you thought they were gone.

Here's a sample prayer if you need some additional support.

Father God, in the name of Jesus Christ, I come to you asking that you heal my brokenness. According to your Word in 1 Peter 5:7, I can cast all of my cares upon you because you care for me. Lord, I am casting this hurt and the memories unto you. Lord, I forgive each person who I've ever felt rejected by, and I thank you for healing my brokenness. Now, Lord, I ask that you help me restore my thoughts so that they are pure so that hat rejection no longer has power in my life. Thank you for healing me, and thank you for the abundance that's to come because I am healed. In Jesus' name, amen.

4. Have uncomfortable conversations.

This is the step that may cause many of you to second guess this process, but I guarantee if you push through, this will be one of the most rewarding moments of your life. During this step, you need to write down every person you ever felt rejected by—whether he/she is deceased or still living, write down the name. Once you've written their names, it's time to have an uncomfortable conversation. It's time for you to go to those people and tell them how they made you feel. Now, I know this can be a little tough, but you can do it. This is why steps one and three require you to seek God in prayer during this process. Addressing the people who rejected you is not a time to get even, cuss them out, tell them what they did wrong or try to hurt them in any way. Check the intent of your heart. This process is so that you can be free; the first step to freedom is courage and forgiveness. If the person is deceased, write them a letter, tell them how you feel, forgive them, and then destroy the letter once you have completed those steps. Why destroy it? Because just as you will never address this matter again with the person who you've felt rejected by, you will not hold on to the letter. Now, what happens if the person you share your feelings with a) rejects or dismisses your feelings again or b) attempts to discredit your point of view or feelings?

You continue to move forward. You've done your part. Everyone around you will not be ready to heal, and you can't force them to. Back in chapter one, you said yes. When you say yes to one thing, you learn the power of your no. If in that moment you start to feel—once again—rejected, you stand on your no and never allow that emotion to hold you captive again.

Visit your past and recall times when you've felt rejected.

    a. Include:

        i. Situations

        ii. Self

        iii. Relationships

        iv. Sporting teams

        v. Parents

        vi. Siblings

        vii. Jobs

        viii. Teachers

        ix. Pastors

        x. Grandparents

        xi. Children

        xii. Friends

        xiii. Relatives

5. Forgive.

Now that the uncomfortable conversations are done, you now have to forgive each person you've listed. Mark 11:25 says, "And whenever you stand praying, forgive, if you have anything against anyone, so that your Father also who is in heaven may forgive your trespasses." Forgiving the person who hurt you is not for the person; it's for you. That's why it's okay if they don't receive your confession with compassion and empathy; this is your process, and this step alone will catapult you into freedom. Forgiveness unlocks so many rewards in business and in life. One thing you'll need to take your business from six-figures to multiple six-figures is a team. If you're struggling with rejection, how will you ever trust someone enough to help take you to your next level?

Before we move forward to exercise six, I want to address the difference between someone telling you "no" and rejection. Your brain doesn't recognize the difference between the two because you've allowed the response to affect you the same way. "No," is a complete sentence. Someone telling you "no" may or may not be a form of rejection. The power of their no may simply be because of their decision to say "yes" in another area. Get to the root of the "no." Understand the reason behind it before you assume it's a dismissal of an idea or you. Review your work guide for additional support.

> **WHERE IS THE "NO" COMING FROM?**
>
> - Lack of understanding
> - Slothfulness
> - Emotionally not prepared or ready to handle the responsibilities of a yes
> - Genuinely uninterested
> - Unable to see it from your point of view
>
> *A rejected "no" stems from a different place.*
>
> - Abandonment
> - Neglect
> - Don't want to believe in your ideas because no one believed in theirs
> - The only way the person knows how to respond
> - They were rejected
> - Jealousy or envy

FIG. 1

Check the intent of the "no." If you've experienced someone telling you "no," unless that person is genuinely uninterested, there could be so many reasons for that answer. Before you take the "no" personally and start to allow your subconscious to remind you of past experiences, you should find the root of the "no."

When a person rejects you or an idea, it most likely comes from a place of being rejected.

- Are you the rejector? Do you reject others because you've been rejected?

- Have you told others "no" for some of the reasons you've identified in fig. 1?

- Do you not tell others "no" because you don't want to reject them and make them feel how you felt?

This exercise is designed to help you change your perspective on how others may have made you feel. I want you to realize that rejection is only a response to being rejected. Understand that you weren't being rejected, it was the rejected person deflecting their hidden emotions onto you. God made you in His image. You were fearfully and wonderfully made; therefore, He accepts you exactly the way that you are. You are good enough, and He loves you. Christ will never reject you; He will receive you wherever you are. God seeks a pure heart not a perfect performance. Know that people-pleasing does not eliminate rejection, it magnifies it.

Then Jesus said, "Come to me, all of you who are weary and carry heavy burdens, and I will give you rest," Matthew 11:28 KJV

6. Research.

I encourage you to stay in prayer for the next 30 days. While this process will require a daily yes from you, you want to make sure you are strengthening your confidence and mindset as you continue to journey forward. Find supportive literature that will help you during your rejection recovery journey. My best recommendation is the Holy Bible, but find books that complement the Word of God so that you can stay focused and on track.

7. Replace your attention.

Now that you've completed exercises 1-6, it's time to shift your attention from the experiences that have caused you emotional pain to the experiences that will create new memories and fulfillment. You're no longer bound by the rejection of others; you are free to create the life you truly want to live through Christ Jesus. While replacing your attention from pain to purpose, I want you to identify how you can help someone else overcome the exact obstacles you've experienced. As we journey through this process, we will discuss strategies to identify your ideal client. Be sure to take notes on how rejection made you feel, what it made you believe, and the behaviors it created. This is research data you already have access to. We can use it later in our process.

8. Be thankful.

Now that you've been healed, let's show gratitude and appreciation towards your new journey. This process doesn't mean the memory won't sting every now and again; it means that you will no longer allow this memory to control your possibilities. Be grateful for your freedom, for the good God has given you, and the better that's to come. If you want to know the secret to pushing forward in your coaching business when thoughts start to slow you down, it's the power of gratitude. An exercise I've found extremely helpful, specifically during the times when my thoughts were distracting me, is writing out the things I'm grateful for. This exercise gives me the opportunity to recognize the things God has done for me in my business and in my life that I may have overlooked. It gives me the chance to be appreciative when I'm feeling stuck in my goals. List what you're grateful for; be sure to thank God for the past, present, and future blessings.

9. Walk in it.

Now that you've completely surrendered your hurt to Christ, it's time to own your transformation. This is your time to walk in confidence and freedom without your past showing up and creating massive roadblocks to keep you stuck. Walking in your healing can seem nearly impossible when you've been stuck in a certain mentality for so long. Still, every day you take an additional step further will bring you one step closer to the true freedom you desire in your business and in Christ. Don't be alarmed; your thoughts and words will be different. People may not understand why or how you've reached such a certain place of clarity and peace, but know it's not for anyone to understand but you. Forgiveness is not for everyone to understand; forgiveness is so that you can walk in the fullness of Christ Jesus and His purpose.

10. Be Accountable.

The one thing we always seem to search for when we're on a journey of healing and forgiveness is the accountability of the offender. But what if I told you that this journey only required you to take accountability for yourself. I know, we want to blame someone, we want the other person to own up to their wrong, but this is your journey. You must be held accountable for your forgiveness so that you no longer allow what the offender did to ever stop you from pushing forward. Own your journey, Don't point the finger, and stop expecting those who have hurt you to own their wrong. They have their own journey to travel. Be accountable for your yes, your decision to forgive, and walk in your healing with confidence.

Step 3

DECIDE THERE ARE NO OTHER OPTIONS

Step 3
DECIDE THERE ARE NO OTHER OPTIONS

Have you ever been told, "Always have a plan B"? I'm sure you have; most of us were taught to always have a plan B in case plan A didn't work. What if I told you that type of thinking will only give you an excuse not to give something all you've got. Why need a backup plan if you're fully committed to His plan? The only reason most people need a plan B is because plan A was their plan and not His plan. You have to decide whether or not coaching is His plan for you or your plan for yourself. Proverbs 16:9 says, "The heart of man plans his way, but the Lord establishes his steps." This simply means you may think you know the plans for yourself and your business, but when you decide to pursue purpose and trust God, the steps in your plans are then ordered by God, which doesn't need an alternate route.

Write down your Plan A. What is it you truly want, and who will it serve? Then write down your plan B, C, etc., and who it will serve. After you've completed a full brain dump, identify why your Plan B, C, D, etc., won't truly work. If you feel like they will all work, then the next nine steps won't help you. Multiple plans mean you don't believe enough in yourself and what God has given you to make the first plan work. When the process becomes difficult, it doesn't mean the plan won't work and that you should abort it. It could mean that you need to readjust the plan until it works. Whether you need to rework your messaging or your mindset, know that distractions or what you may deem difficult, is not a sign to give up. Trust God even more and push forward.

After completing your list, be honest with yourself and identify why you even considered these additional plans. This exercise should help you realize just how important your Plan A is and reveal signs of fear and doubt. Most times, we house backup plans in our subconscious because we're afraid of failure. We prepare ourselves for the "What if this doesn't work?" but I challenge you to reprogram your mindset and only ask yourself, "What if it does?" What if you fail? What if you don't? What If no one hires you? What if your calendar is booked 365 days a year? Preparing for the worse is like showing up to failure before it even happens.

Here are a few wise words I gained from a coaching program in which I was enrolled: "Don't 'what if' down, 'what if' up."

In other words, don't prepare for the worst, prepare for the best. Your best and your worst are both conditional, so you might as well shift that energy towards success.

Deciding there is no other option can feel uncomfortable and go completely against what you've been taught. There is a popular saying, "You should never put all your eggs in one basket," but you only have two hands. One hand to carry the basket (vision) and the other hand to pick the eggs (building the vision). Don't get caught up in the Jack and Jill phenomenon—you know, "Jack and Jill of all trades" because they master at none. They may be good at them, but they never master them.

In this book, I want to help you make a decision and become the expert—the most sought-after coach in the industry. The only way we can reach this goal is if you decide that you're willing to ride Plan A until no other plan is even an option. Now, don't get me wrong, as we move further in the book, we will discuss creating multiple streams of income. However, there's a difference between having multiple streams of income and jumping from industry to industry, trying to be all things to all people. If you're a real estate coach, use your profit from your coaching business to buy property, invest, and build a financial portfolio. Stop trying to coach, sell jewelry, and bake cakes; they don't tie into one another. This type of routine will never establish you as the "go-to" expert and garner the respect you want from the world. If you're going to coach and sell jewelry, make it make sense. Don't advertise that you're a Mindset Coach in one advertisement and then that you sell jewelry in another.

Your decision to go full force into the coaching industry can be so rewarding, but only if you're willing to strap on your boots for the ride. I went full-time in business back in 2014. I had no idea what I was getting myself into, I just knew God had called me to this very unfamiliar place. I was willing to trust Him through it. There were times when I wanted to just throw in the towel and get a "regular job." I was tired of battling with the unfamiliar waters of the coaching industry and being broke while I tried to figure it out. It was exhausting. I had decided I would be committed to the assignment, but I hadn't yet decided that I was willing to endure some of the character-building moments I experienced. As I shared in previous chapters, there was a lot of healing that had to take place in my life before I was ready to commit to the journey fully. Now, don't get me wrong, I have a lot further to go. Because I've decided to be committed to my business—by any means necessary—I'm willing to adjust and change in the areas needed. Are you willing to adapt and change? Visit your digital workbook. Identify areas in your life that could be hindering you from reaching your life goals. Have you totally committed to the process? Are you willing to change in areas where you're most comfortable? You may not see all of the areas immediately that will require change and growth, but you have to be willing to address and adjust them at the surface.

Why should there be no other options? When you've made up in your mind that there are no other options outside of you taking your coaching business from Start to Six-figures, you're training your mind to figure it out. When you feel like you've run into a brick wall, your immediate response is no longer to abort. Now you're focused on how to get over, around, or through the wall. This type of thinking is what will catapult you into six-figures. You're no longer looking for the easiest way out, but the strategies to get you through.

The moment you say "yes" to God, you're deciding, at that moment, there is no other option. Whether that be in business, life, or career, your "yes" to Christ jumpstarts your journey towards abundant living. Joshua 24:15 encourages us to choose who we shall serve. In that decision, you're not only accepting Christ as the Lord and Savior of your life, but you're accepting the assignment that is connected to your choice. If your assignment is local or global, once you've decided to choose Christ and His plans for you, there should be no other option. Don't define "success" according to your wants and desires; your thoughts may be limiting you. Define "success" according to the Word of God, and what He has for you. It'll make your commitment that much stronger.

Step 4

MASTER YOUR MESSAGE

Step 4
MASTER YOUR MESSAGE

Now that we've taken some time to work on your internal, let's focus on the external. When you think of brand messaging, think about your favorite fairytale or childhood book. The story that made you feel warm and fuzzy or scared the life out of you. Recall a story that, when you think of it, takes you back to the place you first heard it. Can you recall that story? As a child, I read the storybook *Greens Eggs and Ham* by Dr. Suess. I've probably read this story 100 times, and with three elementary-aged boys, I'm sure I'm well over 1000. Every time I read this story, it always takes me back to kindergarten. If you know me, then you know my memory isn't the best, but this is an experience I can remember vividly. We were returning to our desks after leaving the multi-colored alphabet rug, and we had just finished *Green Eggs and Ham*. I returned to my corner seat with my name tag taped to the top of my desk and all of my supplies to make our five-year-old version of *Green Eggs and Ham*. The hot plates were going, and the green food dye was being shared graciously. As an adult, green eggs and ham sound pretty gross, but as a five-year-old little girl, it was probably the best meal I had ever had. My kindergarten teacher checks on me from time to time until this day, and I occasionally remind her of that warm and fuzzy experience of making green eggs and ham in her classroom that day.

Why is this story relevant? This, my dear, is the exact experience you want to have when sharing your story with your audience. You want to share a story they will never forget. A story that's relatable. A story that connects the listener to your imagination so they can feel like they were once there. Messaging is the core of your coaching brand, and you want to be sure you're creating a message that's relatable, retainable, and results-driven. In my Niché Certification Program, I help the coaches master their message by helping them discover the message they don't mind reciting for the rest of their career. Your message is what connects your potential client to your solution. Mastering your message can take a little while, especially if you're looking to build an authentic business and share a relatable message. You want your message to be relatable to your audience, and you want your ideal client to know that you were once where they currently are.

HOW TO DISCOVER YOUR MESSAGE?

Here's the point in this 12 Step Process where you're going to have to get real with yourself. Ask yourself this: am I building this business to shift the *moment* for my client or the mindset? If your answer is mindset, then we're going to have a great time digging beneath the surface to truly discover the message God wants you to share. If you only want to shift the moment, then we may want to re-examine your intention behind coaching.

Coaching is an industry designed to help men, women, and children identify the roadblocks that prevent them from reaching the success they desire in life. There is a very distinct line between coaches, counselors, and therapists. Coaches may visit your past to help identify the reasons behind current behaviors, but counselors and therapists will stay there for a while to address concerns and behaviors on a much deeper level. As a coach, you want to identify roadblocks that are stopping the client from moving forward and help the client create strategies to get them to the success they desire.

Most coaches struggle with messaging because they try to create a message that is popular instead of creating a message that is purposeful. If you're trying to build a coaching business based on the most popular niché then you'll never experience the fullness in helping someone solve a problem. Your message should come from within. It should be a mirror of what you've once experienced in your own journey. Take a moment and identify the area(s) in your life where you've experienced something traumatic, and God has healed you. Maybe it wasn't a traumatic experience. Maybe it was a behavior that you found yourself repeating throughout your life, but you never identified it as a gift, even if parents or loved ones told you it was annoying or never nurtured it. Maybe it is a gift or talent that you haven't figured out how to monetize. We want to get to the root of your message and make sure it's connected to your service for others. Get clarity on why you want to help others in the areas you've identified. Make sure the "why" behind your message connects with purpose and not popularity.

We can sometimes get wrapped up in the noise in the world, but stay true to the problem you were called to solve. Your experiences may have seemed painful, but they weren't for you. Your experiences are for the people you're called to serve in your coaching business. God allowed those things to happen so that you can give Him glory through serving others and helping them in areas they aren't strong enough to endure. Maybe you've struggled with confidence, self-love, or forgiveness. Those experiences were designed to make you stronger; that's why you were able to overcome them. Now it's time to take what you've learned, how you were able to overcome, package it, price it, and offer it to your ideal client.

This level of clarity will be the core of your message and will help you create an authentic brand that speaks to the masses. In my Niché Certification Program, I have an exercise that helps the coaches dig deep and find their message using our "why wheel." Your message shouldn't be crafted out of what sounds good or what will make the most money. Your message should be clear, specific, and authentic. Then when it's time to work through your program, copywriting, and marketing, you can deliver from a place of clarity and authenticity. Connecting your "why" to your message also increases your level of commitment. It's proof that the solutions you're offering in your programs work because they're connected to a personal experience.

Once you've identified the "why" and the root in your message, we want to create a power statement that is 30 seconds or less and addresses who you are as a coach, the problem you solve, and the results you can help your ideal client attain. Before we go into your crafting your message, recognize the difference between your message, your power statement, and your content.

WHAT IS MY MESSAGE?

Your message is the story behind the problem you solve and the solutions you help your ideal clients attain. Your message is what connects a person to your brand and compels them to work with you. This is why we want to be sure that your message is clear and authentic. We don't want to craft a message that's manipulating; we want to craft a message that speaks to the heart of your audience and inspires change and transformation.

WHAT IS MY POWER STATEMENT?

Your power statement is a quick 1-2 sentence statement that describes who you are, who you serve, the problem you solve, and the results you bring. Our goal is to create a statement that captures our ideal client's attention and inspires him/her to work with us. This process alone can take a little time. Trying to condense so much into 20 words or less can feel challenging, but it's effective. You have to figure out how to get your ideal client's attention without the need to explain and re-explain what you do time and time again.

I'll give you an example:

I help Christian female startup coaches start, grow, and monetize their coaching business from start to six-figures in their niché.

Now there will be times when you will need to condense this statement with even fewer words. So I challenge you to try and describe what you do in as few words as possible.

WHAT IS CONTENT?

Content is different ways you will share your message; it's story-telling. I encourage the coaches in my community to identify three areas in which they want to be considered an expert. This helps with narrowing down your talk topics and keeping your information consistent. Content can be shared in multiple ways: pictures, posts, blogs, videos, websites, or sales pages. Whatever content that you share, make sure that it's relevant to your message and the problem you solve for your ideal client.

Content creating becomes more simple the more authentic you become in your message. It can begin to feel frustrating when you're trying to be all things to all people. When you're clear on your niché, messaging, and ideal client, your content becomes consistent, precise, and repeatable. Most times, coaches run away from this concept in fear of being repetitive, but think about the

Rule of 7. It takes a person, at minimum, seven times to hear your message before she/he even considers taking action. There is so much research available about this concept; some articles will even argue that a client has to hear your message six to 20 times before investing. As quickly as our world is moving, most people are only retaining about 10% of the content you share. To help your ideal client connect with your content, you need to become repetitive. You may think you've said something 100 times, but there will be people listening or reading your content for the first time. What are the three areas in which you want to be considered an expert as it relates to your message? Identify these three areas and talk about them as often as you can. Be creative. Find new ways to say the same thing over and over again. I watch clients all the time have "aha" moments to something I'm sure I've said 100 times before. Don't make this more complicated than it has to be. Find your lane and ride in it all the way to six-figures. There may be traffic along the way, but be patient; you'll get there.

Step 5

SOLVE A PROBLEM

Step 5
SOLVE A PROBLEM

*I*n the previous steps, we've had the opportunity to cover a lot of groundwork. As we explore the problem you solve in your coaching business, I want you to truly recognize the value you offer to your ideal client. We're going to connect the problem you solve for others to the problem you once had to solve for yourself. This section will separate you from being a traditional life coach and being an expert. As we've identified in the messaging step, examine the experiences in your life that stand out most. Discover the problem that you to had to solve and heal from so that you could reach the next level in life or business.

When I think back on when I first started my coaching business, I was excited to serve my clients in every capacity they needed me. While I was servicing entrepreneurs, I was helping them in many areas of their life. Then after several years of working with both service and product-based entrepreneurs, I started to become overwhelmed. I think I was on an information overload. Every time someone new came to me with an idea they wanted to birth, I had to take out the time to study and learn the industry so that I could offer them the best strategies. That was exhausting. The true struggle didn't surface until I was stuck in my business doing tasks I didn't want to do so that I could barely make money and still be broke. I was struggling. I was struggling financially, and I was struggling with what I was offering to my clients.

During that time, a client reached out and asked me to do a business plan for his restaurant. This is where I drew the line. I absolutely hated this project. I wasn't interested in how restaurants needed to market, or writing the executive summary, or completing the industry analysis—it just drained me. I can remember the conversation between my husband and me. He was so upset that I had turned down a business plan that could have potentially brought us about $3,000 of income because I didn't want to do it. We could have truly used the income. My response to him was, "If I wanted to work a job that I dreaded, I could have stayed at my 9-5." This was a pivoting moment for me and my business. I no longer wanted to do things to bring me money; I wanted to do things that fulfilled God's purpose for my life and made me smile. Business plan writing and coaching every entrepreneur who sought support wasn't doing those things for me.

The problem you solve in your coaching business is deeper than the surface areas we're used to speaking about. When we talk about the problem you solve, I'm referring to the internal conflict that is stopping your client from reaching their next level in life.

Remember when we discussed the differences between a coach, therapist, and counselor? Getting to the root of your client's problem will require you to visit their past, but remember, don't stay there. This is why you should identify the problem in your life first. This will help you recognize the behaviors and beliefs your client is struggling with. When it was time for me to really get to the root of the problem I solved for my ideal client, I experienced a fight. I had to do the internal work that I didn't think was stopping me from hitting my business goals. I know we don't believe that our internal conflicts play a huge part in our success, but they do. We talked about a few of them earlier in this book. Pride and rejection were huge roadblocks in my coaching business, and once I started the healing process, the problem I was called to solve became clear.

Know the difference between the problem you solve and the services you offer. Your services are the "how" to your results; the problem you solve is the "why" behind their struggle. Let's reflect on our coach that we've previously discussed, Mindset Coach. Be clear of the problem you solve for your ideal client. Think it through. For the sake of the book, I wanted to be consistent in the type of coach I used as an example; however, the strategies I've shared can be used for any type of niché coach: Book Coach, Confidence Coach, Wealth Coach, Self-Care Coach and even Vision Coach. When you think about the behaviors that your ideal client is currently experiencing, consider the problem that's causing that behavior? Instead of listing how you're going to help them, help them identify what's causing the mindset barriers.

This is how you're able to address the problem with detail and precision. As a Mindset Coach who helps high-achieving women break free from limiting beliefs so that they can scale their six-figure businesses, you want to help your client identify what caused the limiting beliefs so that you can get to the root of the problem. When you help your client do this, it exposes other areas that may be causing the client to stay stuck. Limiting beliefs are the effects of what problem? What caused your client not to believe in their abilities? After working with you and identifying the problem, your client will navigate other life experiences a lot easier.

Take a moment and ask yourself, "What problem do I solve as a coach?" What is the rooted issue causing your client to be stuck in his/her current thinking pattern? The problem you solve can show up in many different behaviors and beliefs.

WHAT ARE BEHAVIORS AND BELIEFS?

Behaviors are actions that are the result of an internal issue or problem. Beliefs are what the client believes as a result of the internal issue or problem. Once you're able to clearly identify the behaviors and beliefs the problem is causing, you'll find it easier to create marketing copy that speaks directly to your ideal client. If you're familiar with marketing segmentation, then you know that understanding the psychographics of your client takes marketing to a much deeper level. Traditionally, we're taught that identifying the demographics and geographics of your target audience is sufficient. However, after years of studying niché marketing for coaches, I've learned that understanding the psychographics of your ideal client makes marketing your program and connecting to your ideal client a lot easier.

Let's reflect on your message. When we identified your message based on your life experiences, examine the behaviors and beliefs you had during that experience and write it down. Next, identify the problem that caused those behaviors and beliefs. Now that you've decided there are no other options but to stay committed to your coaching journey, let's walk step by step up until this point:

1. Identify your message, the area in which you want to support others. Make sure this message connects to a personal experience so that we can ensure authenticity and purpose.

2. Once you've identified the message, identify the behaviors and beliefs that you want to help your client overcome during your relatable experience.

3. Now, identify the problem that caused those behaviors and beliefs. This is the problem you solve in your coaching business.

When I sat down to complete this exercise for myself, I learned that the rooted problem to many of my life experiences was lack of confidence and the need for validation. These things were rooted in the relationship between my father and me and the bullying I experienced in grade school. I learned that there was a difference between being strong and pushing through and actually healing. I was strong enough to push through, but these areas began to resurface in my adult life and in my business. That's when I learned that I needed to be more than just strong—I needed to heal. My healing process is what catapulted my coaching business. I was freed from limiting thinking, depression, doubt, and imposter syndrome once I completely surrendered my hurt to Christ and asked Him to lead me. Where do you need healing? What deep-rooted issue are you holding on to or sweeping under the rug, denying the fact that it still affects you? You'll find it extremely difficult to be authentic with your clients if you're still having a hard time personally. Which problem are you called to solve? What have you struggled with most?

Let's use the example of the Mindset Coach I discussed earlier in the chapter. The behaviors that her client is currently experiencing are limiting beliefs. Keep in mind, limiting beliefs are the behaviors, not the actual problem. Now let's discover the problem that caused the limiting beliefs. What has this Mindset Coach personally experienced that caused limiting beliefs within herself? Remember, when we start to examine the ideal client we want to recognize how it was present in our own lives. Could it be rejection? Or childhood abandonment? Remember, our goal is to change our ideal client's mindset, not just change the moment. By getting to the root, our client can identify other areas this problem may try to show up in and because we've created strategies that will pull the problem from the root, when this problem attempts to show in other areas of her life the client will know how to get through them. This is true transformation.

The problem you solve in your coaching business may or may not be obvious in your messaging or to the client. I don't usually put the problem I solve in my written content, but you'll find me talking about it in a live training from time to time. Sharing that the problem I solve is lack of confidence and validation may not be as easily received as it would be with me sharing it in a training. Of course, lack of confidence is pretty self-explanatory, but validation can be a little tricky. You can share the problem you solve in your messaging, or you can share it in your program. It's really up to how you position your messaging.

Most times, when people hire a coach they know what they want, but they don't know what they need. They are just unsure of what's stopping them from getting what they want in life. There is a possibility that the client isn't ready to admit to certain problems they are experiencing that could be the reason for their inability to move forward. This is why we share the problem in our program after we've completed a series of exercises that reveal it. The client may think her hang-up is limiting beliefs. Really, her issue is that as a child, she struggled with rejection from her father, which created limiting beliefs. Be creative with how you address the problem so that it doesn't scare the client away, or so that it doesn't feel like she's in a therapy session—especially if it's something she didn't know would resonate. I reframe from using the term "validation" in my marketing because when people see this word, they automatically assume it's the need for approval from others. Instead, I help people accept their coaching gift regardless of anyone else's approval. One of my favorite scriptures I share with the coaches in my program is Matthew 18:19, "Where two should ask anything in my father's name here on earth, then it shall be done." His Word is all the validation you need!

Step 6

NICHÉ MARKETING FOR CHRISTIAN COACHES

Step 6
NICHE MARKETING FOR CHRISTIAN COACHES

How much do you know about niché marketing? When you hear the word "niché" what do you think of? Do you think "limiting" or "inability to grow"? Is there a little fear there when you think about narrowing your coaching business down to solve a specific problem for a specific group of people? In the last step, we identified the problem you solve in your coaching business, which will connect to an essential piece of what we will discuss in this step. Discovering your niché is not about limiting your reach; it's more about magnifying your message. Your niché is what separates you from other coaches in the industry and what establishes you as the expert in solving a specific problem. I know you're thinking there are other coaches who are building their businesses in your same niche. Your niché is what separates you in the industry, but your message is what helps you stand out. Your niché may be similar, but your message is uniquely crafted and can only be shared by you.

When you think of Niché Marketing, I want you to think of the area you want to establish your expertise. What do you want to be known for? What problem will you solve, and whose problem will you solve? When you go to your family practitioner with a foot issue, he won't help you solve that issue; he sends you to a pediatrist. Why? Because your family practitioner isn't an expert in feet. It doesn't mean he couldn't give you a diagnosis or tell you what the problem could be, it means that he wouldn't be operating in his expertise. So why do you keep trying to operate outside of your area of expertise? Would you go to your dentist to fix your eye issue?

The reason you operate outside of your area of expertise is because you don't consider yourself an expert. We've been conditioned to believe that an expert is someone of higher primacy, deemed academically and economically superior. We assume a person who refers to herself as an expert must have years of education, experience, and field study. She is a person who is well versed in a particular area of study and is validated by someone in some superior position. What if I told you that you fit every requirement of an expert? Let's break it down.

1. **Years of education** – How long was your healing process? Remember, our message is crafted from the exact thing from which God healed us. What did you have to do to heal and grow? This process didn't just happen overnight for you; it took studying, wisdom and application.

2. **Experience** – revisit the experiences that qualified you to speak from a space of healing and breakthrough. You can't learn this type of experience in a book. You've been healed, set free, and delivered from some traumatic experiences that no textbook could ever share. Your experiences weren't about you; God designed them for the people you will impact and serve. You can't pay for the experiences you've had, but someone should pay for the solutions you have to help them get through the things you've conquered. Whether your experiences were traumatic, uncomfortable, difficult, or just non-traditional, you experienced them, and no one can tell you how significant or insignificant your experiences were but you. Someone is going through the exact thing you've experienced. You may think it's simple to get through it, but someone is struggling. That conquered experience that you have in common with that person is stopping them from being great.

3. **Field Study** – Now that you've been healed and free in this area, how many times has something come up that reminded you of that experience? How many times did you push through without allowing your past to weigh you down and keep you stuck? Your practical execution of your internal healing has changed your outcome in life. Not only has it changed you, but you can see certain behaviors and patterns in other people's lives that remind you of the

problem you once had, which then ignites the desire for change in that person.

4. **Superiority Validation-** If this is what God has called you to do, then His validation is all you need.

Stop underestimating your brilliance because someone else hasn't called you brilliant. Christ called you brilliant the day you were born; everything He creates is brilliant. It's life that convinces us otherwise. Many of you may be reading this and automatically disqualifying yourself from showing up as the expert because you're belittling your life's experiences. Healing doesn't have to be this exaggerated experience that's only applicable to people who've experienced traumatic hurt, pain, or illness. Healing is the moment your perspective shifts from one way of thinking to another. Think about the woman with the issue of blood (Matthew 9:20-22). She wasn't healed because she physically touched Jesus' hem; she was healed because of her belief. She was healed the moment she said it, not after she touched Him. Her faith made her whole. Once your perspective shifts from victim to victor, healing starts. The moment you stopped being the victim, the moment you stopped letting your circumstances dictate your outcome, the moment you decided you would never return to that place that kept you stuck, bound, or hurt, you were healed.

Don't choose a niché because it's profitable or popular; choose a niché because of its purpose. The key to your six-figure year is narrowing down the problem you solve and becoming crystal clear on your ideal client. Most times, coaches struggle with being niché specific because our natural response to business is to get as many clients as we can instead of working with the clients we're called to serve. The specification of your niché is what attracts your ideal client. The more specific you are, the clearer you become in the industry and the higher your demand.

IT STARTS WITH YOUR TITLE

This is probably my favorite topic to discuss. Your first two forms of marketing for your coaching business before you even open your mouth are your title and your power statement. Your power statement describes who you are, who you serve, the problem you solve, and the results you bring. Your title should be a direct reflection of the problem you solve for your ideal client. It should describe the type of transformation you will help your client achieve while working with you. Your title is a form of marketing; it either speaks directly to your ideal client or confuses them. When selecting your title as a coach, you want to use one adjective to describe yourself. Once you start to layer the adjectives in your title, it can confuse your audience.

Let's look at our example coach, who I mentioned earlier: a Mindset Coach. Imagine seeing her market her business as a Mindset Empowerment Coach. Two things come to mind: will she help me with my mindset or empower me to do something? You have about 30 seconds to capture the attention of a potential client. The moment I have to wonder whether or not you're talking to me is the moment you lose me. Don't make your audience work. Be specific, be simple, be clear. Yes, our Mindset Coach will help you shift your mindset and create wealth, but the problem she's called to solve is the mindset. The results of a shifted mindset will bring you wealth. Instead of trying to appeal to everyone—assuming the word "empowerment" will capture their attention—we can focus on the problem and put the results inside of the power statement.

Mindset Coach (name), empowering high-achieving women to break free from limited beliefs so that they can scale a six-figure business. In her marketing, she can address the behaviors of a broken mindset, and her ideal client will know that she is speaking directly to her problem. Coaching is the service you provide; the adjective is the problem you solve.

Layering your title is unnecessary when your power statement is clear. It is also an indication that you are not confident in the problem you solve or the person you're called to serve in your business. Most times, coaches layer their titles because they want to appeal to more people. Saying you're a Mindset Empowerment Coach may sound deep and intellectual, but it requires too much thinking on the audience side. The best marketing strategy is a simple one. Don't crowd your expertise with a bunch of titles. Your ideal clients want to know that you can do one of four things: save them time, save them money, help them lose weight, or create happiness in their lives. Not only do they want to know if you can help them, but how you can help them without needing to do extensive research to figure how you can help them. Your title should describe the problem you solve. Your power statement should describe how, who it's for, and the results you bring.

PROFIT FOR TRANSFORMATION

When you choose entrepreneurship, you're most familiar with two major forms of sales: profit for product and profit for service. What if I told you there was a third sales area that isn't shared on Google? This area of sales is where coaches thrive. Profit for transformation. Exchanging profit for transformation is where you remove the limits off how much you can charge for your coaching services. We research the going rate for consultants and goods, but when you enter into the area of transformation, the limits are removed because there is no fair monetary investment on how your transformation strategies can affect a person. Think about it: the strategies you will implement to help transform the mindset of your clients aren't just strategies that will affect them, they will also affect those around and connected to them. It will affect how they do life, work, business, and parenting. The transformation will affect generations. This is why we want to make sure we're grounded in the Word of God because what you teach and the intent behind what you teach doesn't stop at the paid invoice or when the coaching term is up. You want to be sure you're depositing sound wisdom and strategy that is rooted in Christ. Now, how do you measure that type of value? This is why you need to believe and value your worth so that you're offering your solutions at an investment that encourages growth, change, and sustainability for both you and the client.

When entering into the coaching industry, we may assume coaching is the exchange of profit for service. We associate the services we offer our clients with business services we see others provide, but when coaching becomes a lifestyle, it becomes more than a service. It becomes a unique space to support others in a lifestyle transformation. Services include what the client will get "while working" with you, transformation is what the client will get "because of working" with you. When you consider your coaching transformation, it strengthens your confidence in other areas of your life and business that will determine whether you grow or fail. Areas such as pricing, programing, and packaging are established at a certain level based on your mindset and your desire to transform. Your "yes" to coaching is bigger than what you've assumed. Until you take it as seriously as it is, you'll continue to find yourself struggling to create a business that generates the profit you desire and impacts the people you're called to serve. You want to speak to the problem that eliminates the behavior through the services you provide.

CHASING PROFIT INSTEAD OF PURPOSE

Over the 17 years I've been in business, I've transitioned from entrepreneurship to self-employed to business owner and learned a lot about the marketing industry. My entrepreneurship season was when I was trying to figure it out while working a job on the side. I started several businesses. I was what I considered to be a serial entrepreneur: trying to go with what brought in cash and chasing profit instead of purpose. Ironically enough, even in those endeavors, purpose would still burst out of me because I've always loved serving and supporting people. I entered the self-employed season when I transitioned from a "dual-preneur" (working my 9-5 and my business) into full-time entrepreneurship. This was the season when I truly learned the grit of business building. I learned so many lessons and cried so many tears, but going back to a traditional 9-5 wasn't an option. I knew that If I was able to generate $20,000 a year in my business, I could generate $2,000,000 a year. I just needed to figure out the formula. By this time, God had shown me the pieces; I just needed to figure out how to put them together. This is where my first coach came into play.

This was the season when I entered Step 3— I decided there were no other options. Step 3 was long for me. I had hired myself as an employee of the business and was completing every position of the company. This was tough and one of the reasons I stayed stuck for as long as I did. Although I had decided there were no other options, the mental roadblocks that were keeping me stuck (pride, rejection, validation) weren't clear. I hadn't realized they were huge distractions in my growth. My moment of transformation was when I invested in my first coaching program, and "boom!" This program introduced healing and deliverance to me in business like I had never seen. I was used to deliverance in church, but I had no idea it played such an intricate part in business. This was when the transformation started. I went through layer after layer, pruning those things that were blinding me from the path God had called me to. I started to invest in myself and my business. My mindset began to change about money. I wanted more; therefore, I knew more was required of me. I became a business owner after years of being on Step 3, finally mastering Step 4, realizing the significance of Step 5, and establishing myself as an expert in Step 6. Once you've transitioned into the season of business ownership, your focus changes. We will talk more about scaling and hiring a team later; I just wanted to introduce to you the different layers of business growth so that you can determine where you are truly going. Everyone isn't called to entrepreneurship, but every entrepreneur who is called is called to be a business owner. It's up to them to decide that there is no other option.

NICHÉ MARKETING FOR COACHES

Traditional marketing is the action of selling a particular service or product. This is what most of us learn when we first start a business. Start your business, file the proper business papers with your state, and sell your product or services. Sounds easy, doesn't it? Niché marketing is a strategy that focuses on a specific audience. This is a strategy that is encouraged by entrepreneurs who want to narrow down their audience and only sell to a select demographic. This form of marketing is traditionally practiced when you're selling a product. I want to introduce a marketing term that I have learned since growing my coaching business into a multiple six-figure business—niché marketing for coaches. This form of marketing is a strategy that focuses on a specific problem and an ideal client. It enhances the relationship between coach and client. It targets a very specific kind of client: one who is mentally prepared to invest and ready to change. Niche marketing for coaches speaks directly to the ideal client; it focuses on the quality of the problem you solve rather than the quantity of problems you solve.

Marketing isn't just about getting people to buy. It's about storytelling and getting people to connect through relatable experiences, feelings, and desires. Later we will talk more about storytelling and how to create a six-figure story map that will navigate your ideal client from where they are to where they desire to be. In the meantime, let's explore the five different niché marketing areas for coaches and determine which one you're currently implementing in your business.

#1 The Layer of Explore – Target Unknown

This layer is where most new and aspiring coaches start. There is zero income but a lot of excitement and fear. She wants to coach and impact lives and is exploring how to build a six-figure coaching business. She's afraid to be specific and wants to coach anyone willing to pay. Her audience isn't clear about what she does or how she can help them. She's casting her net, hoping to catch a fish. She is committed to sharing her message with whoever will listen and wants to pour as much information as possible.

#2 The Layer of Expose – Target Market

This layer is for the coach who is trying to figure out her signature message. She's showing up to increase her on-line visibility and expose her brand to what she has identified to be her target audience through traditional marketing strategies. She shows up, but not consistent enough for her audience to commit. The market she is targeting is aware of her services but not engaged. This coach is trying to speak to everyone in her messaging and is currently using Google for most of their marketing strategies.

#3 The Layer of Engage – Target Audience

Congratulations! This layer is for the coach who has some idea of who she's talking to in her marketing. She's completed her avatar and is familiar with the demographics and geographics marketing segmentations. Her audience is engaged, but they haven't committed to buying just yet. She's made money in her coaching business, but nothing close to what she truly desires. She's worked with a coach or enrolled into a program to help her with her business growth, but she still hasn't reached her income goals. She has a solid message, but it still isn't clear enough to reach the type of client she truly wants to work with.

Do the first three marketing layers sound familiar? Which layer have you identified with? We can find the first three layers in the traditional marketing language. Let's now explore two additional marketing layers.

#4 The Layer of Establish- Ideal Client

This layer is for the coach who is clear of her message and ideal client. She has established a relationship with her audience.

She's invested in a coach who has helped her generate income, but she hasn't been able to generate as consistently as she'd desire. Her audience is committed and engaged with her content and message. She has generated income and is now ready to increase her price point and hit six-figures in her coaching business.

#5 The Layer of Exchange – Enrolled Client

This layer is for the coach who is clear of her message, ideal client, and pricing. She is now exchanging her value and expertise for money. She's enrolled in high-end mastermind classes and is growing her business with ease. She has created a scalable business and is no longer contributing countless hours trying to produce. She has a team and is scaling her business seven figures and beyond.

If you've noticed, when I'm referring to your market, I refer to them as your ideal client. I want to help you learn how to tailor your copy to the one person with whom you truly desire to work. We will discuss more of your ideal client in the next step.

Are you familiar with the term "copy"? Copy is marketing communication in written form to your ideal client, persuading your client to invest in your program. It's how you describe your coaching offer in your marketing content. In your copy is where you share relatable experiences, client testimonies, and how you can help your client. The more clear you are in your messaging, the easier it is to create copy that can be repurposed and shared on multiple platforms.

I shared the different marketing stages in layers instead of steps for a reason. As you journey through your coaching business, you will find yourself experiencing each one of the layers. When something is presented in steps, you assume, with the right information or strategy, you can skip steps. However, skipping steps doesn't mean the process will move quicker. I present these marketing stages in layers because I want you to think of your process like baking a cake. You can't skip steps in baking a cake; every layer is necessary if we're going to produce a masterpiece. The layers that we reviewed are necessary. In every layer, there is something new to learn about you and your business that will help you become a better and stronger coach in the next layer. Now, this doesn't mean you have to spend a certain length of time in each layer. Your progression is based on the effort you put into building a six-figure coaching business and the willingness to shift in your thinking. The layers aren't to be timed stamped but to be a reflection of your growth and clarity. Which layer are you currently in? What do you need in your business to move forward and enter into your next layer? Strong layers build sturdy foundations.

Consider the parable in Matthew 7:24-27; this story reminds me of the children's story *The Three Little Pigs*. Jesus' explained the difference between the wise man who built his house upon stone and the one who built his house upon sand. Which one do you think the wind took down? We want to ensure you are building a coaching business on solid ground; therefore as you grow in your number of clients and revenue, you're building a ground that will sustain you.

DISCOVER YOUR NICHÉ

Your niché is what will help you stand out in the industry and establish yourself as the expert in solving a particular problem. When finding the right niche, you don't want to look for what's popular or profitable. Your niché should be authentic and relevant to the problem you solve in life. As we continue to explore niché marketing for coaches, I will share insight in a very non-traditional way. However, this insight is what has helped me take my coaching business from start to six-figures to multiple six-figures. When finding your niché, I challenge you to do some internal work. Niché marketing forces you to look within and face the very areas that may have caused you pain and trauma.

Many people struggle with facing their past hurt, especially when it causes them to relive that moment and relive those experiences. I get it; this is why healing is necessary on your journey to becoming a six-figure coach. Your niché is the marketing strategy to exposing and fulfilling your life's purpose through coaching. Niché is often referred to as being very specific and different from others. Your coaching lane is very different from others regardless of how many coaches you feel are connected to the same niché you've discovered.

I believe your purpose was uniquely assigned to you at the moment of conception. Jeremiah 1:5 says, "Before I formed you in the womb I knew you, and before you were born I consecrated you; I appointed you a prophet to the nations." This scripture is evidence that God's purpose for your life was uniquely crafted before you were even born. He knew exactly what He wanted from you. Your life's experiences are evidence that God has called and healed you in specific areas so that he can use you to be a conduit of healing in the lives of others. Your niché is a specific problem you solve for a specific person. What was the problem you've identified to solve in the lives of your ideal client? Examine their behavior. The behavior is evidence that a spiritual problem exists. Your niché focuses on that problem and allows you to set yourself apart from other coaches. Not only is it important for you to separate yourself in the industry, but it's vital for you to be specific about your ideal client. The more specific you are, the more your message magnifies.

Mindset Coach (name), empowering high-achieving women to breakfree from limited beliefs...

Can you see how we were specific to what type of woman she wants to work with? Why is this a money-making strategy? When you put "high achieving" to describe the type of woman you want to serve, you attract a different type of client. You attract the client that is ready to invest in her change. The wording you use in your title, and power statement will attract a certain type of client. If you want a client who will invest four-figures or more into your program your, wording is the first step. Of course, we want to provide value and transformation, but your words are what will attract your ideal client. Your processes are what will transform them.

Step 7

KNOW YOUR IDEAL CLIENT

Step 7
KNOW YOUR IDEAL CLIENT

Throughout this book, I put an emphasis on your ideal client. I want you to get into the habit of speaking directly to the ideal client in your marketing instead of the target audience. Here's something unique about the marketing layers I shared: when your ideal client first comes into contact with your content, she is a part of your target market. As your content matures and becomes more relevant in her life, she will shift from being apart of your target market to the target audience. The reason I encourage you to make this shift in your messaging is because as you learn how to speak to your ideal client, your copy becomes personal to the client. Most times, when we speak to an *audience*, our language is crafted to a group of people. When you speak directly to a *person*, you often use different terminology and emotion. Throughout this section, clarify your ideal client and learn why knowing your ideal client beneath traditional marketing layers is important.

In the beginning stage of building your coaching business, I'm sure you've Googled strategies on how to market your coaching business to your target market. We're encouraged to identify their demographics and geographics and to create a client avatar that describes who you want to serve in your business. How many of you created an avatar and gave it a name? In my coaching program, I share my ABC identity chart that encourages the coach to identify 26 detailed facts about their avatar so that they can get clarity on who they are to serve in their coaching business. To access the ABC identity chart, **visit www.starttosixfigures.com.** My avatar's name is Mindy, who soon evolved into my ideal client. Although I know Mindy's marital status, salary, and education, I needed to know a little more about her other than her hobbies and where she works to effectively speak to Mindy in my copy. Getting to the root of your ideal client will require some internal work on your behalf. Why do you think steps 1-3 of this book are all internal work? To market like an expert, you must know your client, their current struggles, behaviors, and beliefs. When identifying your ideal client, you want to have a clear understanding of who they are and what they are currently struggling with. When I first started my coaching business, I wanted to coach everyone. Anyone with an idea. I found myself having a hard time connecting with the person I truly wanted to work with. Your ideal client is a reflection of who you once were and the obstacles you've once had to face. Who do you know better than yourself? This is how I concluded that my ideal client is a Christian female startup coach who wants to financially grow her coaching business doing the exact thing God gifted her to do. I was once her, struggling with the exact things I help my clients accomplish in their business. I teach my clients that what you are called from is the very thing you're being called to. You don't have to go and search for your ideal clients; they're currently experiencing what you've overcome.

Your internal work is not only freeing for you, but it's market research for your ideal client. As my coaching business began to grow, I thought I desperately needed a marketing consultant to come into the company and help me get clients. It was a frustrating journey, but the more I learned about niché marketing and peeled back the layers in my personal life, the more clients I gained. It wasn't that I needed to hire a marketing consultant; I needed to learn how to speak to my ideal client through my messaging from my past experiences. It would have been a waste of resources to hire a marketing consultant, and I wasn't clear of my message. Self-discovery was my first breakthrough in learning who I was called to serve and support in my coaching business. The freer I became of my past experiences and the strongholds that were placing limiting beliefs in my thoughts, the more transparent and vulnerable I became in my messaging. Your ideal client is more like you than you know; until you're willing to do the work for yourself, you'll continue to attract clients you don't find fulfilling—or you won't attract clients at all. Be the coach who finds purpose in what you do and not just profit.

AVATAR VS. IDEAL CLIENT

Your avatar and your ideal client are not the same people.

I know, don't shoot the messenger. The avatar is who you think you should work with based on market research. Your ideal client is who you want to work with, based on client and personal experiences. It's the person who fits the three major characteristics of an ideal client:

1. Investing Mindset

2. They see value in your strategies

3. They have an undeniable desire to change

Once you begin to see your past behaviors and beliefs in your current client, it is a significant identifier that it may be your ideal client. Even if she isn't ready to invest, through consistent content and marketing she will soon transition from the target audience layer to the enrolled client layer. In some arenas in the coaching industry, you'll see influencers use the term "dream client" versus "ideal client." I've even heard "soulmate client," but that's way too personal for me. I opt out of using the term "dream client" because I'm a firm believer that words have power. Your words are the product of your thoughts. Most times, when people share their dreams, they are sharing what has either happened while they were sleeping or a wish they hope comes true in the future. A dream is even described as something that you envision but will never achieve. Why would we want to connect the people we want to serve and impact to the deeply rooted definition of a dream stored in our subconscious? Can we re-program our subconscious? Absolutely, but an ideal client is someone ideal for your program. A dream client sounds like something you wish for that may never come to pass. Your words are important; choose them with the outcome in mind.

When crafting your marketing strategies, the number one thing you want to be crystal clear about is what your ideal client needs from you. Then you need to pay attention to the behaviors that are evidence that they need you. Lastly, learn how to speak to them without pointing out their imperfections, which may cause them to retract from working with you. Your ideal client is more than the market research you've discovered by asking people questions about what they need and what they enjoy doing. Your ideal client's needs are a lot deeper. Depending on the problem you will help her solve, getting her to realize you can help may take a little more work. The more you show up and share your expertise, the more your message will connect and persuade them to change. When gaining clarity on your ideal client, examine the behaviors and beliefs preventing them from reaching their goals. "How do we do this?" you ask? Great question. Throughout this entire book we've talked about your healing process and the experiences that have landed you here in the coaching industry. Your ideal client is a direct reflection of who you once were. If you're struggling with identifying the behaviors and beliefs of your ideal client, it's probably because you haven't decided to heal in your personal life. Once you find your ideal client in you, showing up as the expert and creating marketing copy that speaks directly to the client will become a lot easier and less overwhelming. You're overwhelmed with attracting the right clients because you haven't gained enough clarity on who your ideal client is, what they are currently struggling with and their behaviors and beliefs aren't clearly identified. If you're wondering what your ideal client needs from you right now, ask yourself what you needed in the moment you were in the middle of your stuck.

Let's walk through five mini-tasks that will help you gain better clarity of your ideal client:

1. Define how the problem you solve for others has shown up in your personal life.

2. List the behaviors this problem caused in your life.

3. List the behaviors this problem is causing in your ideal client's life.

4. List the beliefs this problem encouraged in your life.

5. List the beliefs your ideal client currently has because of this problem.

One thing you'll notice with this exercise is how similar you are to your ideal client. Once you begin to heal in the area(s) you will serve and support your clients in, you'll begin to see pieces of yourself in your client. This makes your signature strategy a lot easier to implement, and it increases your confidence. When you can see some of your previous behaviors and beliefs manifest in your ideal client, your confidence will skyrocket. Seeing your personal growth will only heighten your expectations and confidence in the growth of your ideal client. Let's use this book as an example. I am excited to share this information with you because I know that if you implement it, you will break personal barriers, grow in your business, change the way you think about money, and reach your six-figure goal in your business. I am sure of this process because it worked for me, and while coaching is no cookie-cutter industry, with the right mindset and an outline of how to move forward, you're sure to win in business. Find the problem in yourself and then work your way into the lives of those who may not have your resources or your tenacity to push through. Matthew 7:3-4 asks, "How can you pull the speck out of someone else's eye when you have a beam in your own?" Solving a problem you've experienced creates relatability and trust between you and your client. It gives you an advantage in your marketing and adds value to your credibility and expertise. When you address your client from a space of experience, it increases their trust, and they are more willing to invest in your strategies.

Your ideal client is waiting for you to show up with strategies that will help them go from where they are to where they truly desire to be in life. Your story and messaging are what will attract them to you. The way you position your messaging is what will determine whether or not they will invest four-figures or more into your solutions. The language you use in your messaging can determine the type of client you attract. I don't want you to go out and get super wordy in your power statement or think it has to sound super intellectual. Be clear, simple, and specific;

however certain words will attract a certain caliber of client. Adjust your words and your pricing to the level of client you desire to work with. Think back to when you were creating your avatar. When you arrived at the salary section, what did you put? I've worked with coaches who desired to serve and support a demographic of people where economic status was low. My recommendation was to create a non-profit to support people who may not be in the economic space to invest four-figures into a coach. Identify a person who has the flexibility in his or her income to invest. You have to think about whether or not your client will invest $1000 into a coach or to feed her family. It's a harsh reality, but it's a reality we have to face if our income goal exceeds $9,000 per month, which will put us on the fast track to six-figures. Find an organization where you can give back your time, start a non-profit, and get grant money for scholarship opportunities. You can't expect a specific investment from a demographic of people who aren't willing or able to invest. Your gift in coaching isn't just to serve and impact; it's to build financial sustainability for your family.

Step 8

TELL THE STORY; DON'T SELL THE SERVICE

Step 8
TELL THE STORY; DON'T SELL THE SERVICE

One of the most critical aspects of marketing is knowing how to tell your story in a way that connects with your ideal client and inspires them to change. This is another reason why it's important for you to truly understand the problem that God designated you to solve in your coaching business and make sure that it connects with a problem you've once had to solve in your life. Storytelling is learning how to connect with your audience and share relatable experiences using language to attract them to your messaging. Learning how to tell your story and not sell your service will require a lot of practice. This is why your niché should be purpose-driven and not profit-driven. When it's time to tell your story, you can speak from a space of authenticity and not manipulation. Your emotions will show through your storytelling; connect with your audience by telling a story that truly transformed your life.

TYPES OF SELLING

When creating copy for your offer, engage with your audience by sharing your similarities. When you get into sharing your services before telling your story, you risk losing a potential client. They are not interested in the services you have, but how you will help transform their life. Your audience wants to know that you understand where they are and that you can help them go from where they are to where they desire to be. Give your ideal client security that you're able to help solve their problem. Stop trying to teach and train in areas in which you are not fluent. Be well versed in who you are, the problem you solve, and the results you're able to help your client gain due to your first-hand experience.

When telling your story, be aware of three major types of selling:

1. Purposeful selling is an intentional connection between you and a potential client. This can be done on social media, a networking event, or when you speak before an audience. When telling your story, use language to attract your ideal client, and share a relatable story that connects you to the client. This form of selling encourages you to create a conversation with your potential client, which is concluded with a call action. With purposeful selling, it may take a little time to create genuine dialogue. You want the client to know that it's more than money but a mindset shift. Be patient. Get to know the potential client and

what she needs. Make sure what she needs is what your program offers.

2. Passive selling is a form of selling when we post on social media or use some form of advertisement to share what we offer in word-form, also followed by a call to action. This form of selling has little to no contact with you. It's designed for people who are ready to buy, whether it's a high-end or low-end offer. They have access to a link to buy. Passive selling can be used for both pre-recorded and live coaching programs, trainings, and products.

3. Painful selling is what I call "the vacuum salesman" or the "mall kiosk guy." The person who comes and knocks on your door or stops you in the mall and tries to sell you something you did not ask for. This type of selling is done a lot on social media when people message you with their pitch. Don't be the vacuum salesman. Create a conversation, as stated in purposeful selling. Makes sure you understand your clients' needs and share how you can better support them.

BE PURPOSEFUL

Storytelling is knowing how to incorporate purposeful selling into your messaging. You don't want your potential client to feel pressured or bombarded with your sales pitch; you want them to feel a connection so that the investment is a no-brainer. Recall your favorite childhood story. Remember, back in step one I shared a childhood memory about *Green Eggs and Ham* by Dr. Suess. Now think about your favorite story. Who were the characters, and what was the problem in the story? How did the characters display the problem, and what were their behaviors? *Green Eggs and Ham* is such a perfect illustration of purposeful selling. All Sam did at the beginning of the story was walk past the cat with a message. Although the cat wasn't committed to the message, it caught his attention. Sam wanted to introduce the cat to something new, and he did this by making his message visible. Although the cat resisted— something our clients do to us all the time— he eventually saw the value. Sam introduced the same product in many different ways until eventually, the cat was ready to buy. Of course, we don't want to nag our potential clients or try to coerce them into investing in something they are not ready for. This will leave you in a struggling relationship by trying to get someone to do something he/she is not ready to do. However, you do want to learn how to tell your story in different ways so that your client connects. You don't want to tell different stories every time; you want to learn how to tell the same story so that it speaks to your audience in a different way. This type of strategy is how you're able to stay consistent in your content.

WHAT'S YOUR STORY?

When we learn about storytelling in a professional space, it is mostly during a public speaking experience. I want to help you tell your story anytime there's an opportunity to connect with a potential client. If you're posting on social media, going live, sending emails, or using advertisements, your story will connect people to your program. In storytelling, be relatable, use personal experiences, and relate them to your ideal client. What similarities do you have? How can you assure them that you've experienced what they are currently going through? This technique gives your ideal client comfort that you have proven strategies in the problem they are currently experiencing. Your story should include something that is retainable. What will help your client remember you? How can you stand out in your storytelling that will cause your ideal client to remember you when she is experiencing a problem you can solve?

Make sure to also include results. You've shared your relatable story, included some way for them to remember you, now share how your process yielded results. Your story should express your why—why are you so passionate about helping someone solve a problem? You don't have to say why you're passionate in every form of communication, but the way you structure your story should reflect passion and purpose.

Finally, your story should be repetitive. Sharing the same story in different ways makes your target audience feel like they know you. It makes your ideal client trust you. It makes your enrolled client stay connected and refer others. Being consistent in your storytelling builds trust and integrity with your audience. When they show up to an event where you are the keynote speaker, and they're able to connect to the same story they've heard before but in a new and innovative way, it makes them feel like they know you personally. That's the type of storytelling experience you want to create every time your audience hears why they should work with you.

Let's take a moment and explore your story by creating a personalized six-figure story map.

1. How can you relate to your ideal client? What have you experienced that they are currently experiencing?
2. How did your experiences make you feel?
3. What did your experiences cause you to believe?
4. What changed?
5. Why did it change?
6. What were the results once you decided to change?
7. How did it change your life?
8. How do you feel now?

Using this outline to tell your story will help you connect better with your audience and inspire your ideal client to work with you. In this industry, we have to be authentic and creative so that we can stand out. Once you've shared your story, conclude it with a client testimonial and call to action. Your call to action is how your client can press buy once she has personally connected to your story. Whether it's to jump on a sales call, a discover/clarity call, to access your lead magnet, or a direct link to buy, lead them to you without having to shuffle through your website. Let me answer this question while you're thinking about it: are websites obsolete? No, but they are no longer the immediate "go-to." I like to consider your website to be your house. It's where you house your information and contact, but your social media and sales pages are the next "go-to."

Your storytelling skill will evolve over time. The more you tell it, the more creative you will get. The beauty of telling your own story is that you can get as personal as you want. There are no limits on what you can say about yourself. Be mindful of who you include in your stories out of respect for others who may be connected to this story in some way, but no one can take your story away whether they agree with it or not. No one can tell you how to feel or how to heal. This process is between you and God. Go into prayer and ask the Holy Spirit to help you tell the story He wants you to tell. Share how He's healed you and be unapologetic about it. Over the years of building my coaching business, I've learned that people will have something to say, but it can't change what you believe. Your faith in Christ and confidence in your gift will take you further than any popular or profitable niché could ever take you. It's because of you that you're amazing, and your coaching gift is valuable. You were fearfully and wonderfully made in the image of God (Psalms 139:14); therefore everything about you is magnificent and should be valued as such.

Step 9

MAKE AN OFFER

Step 9
MAKE AN OFFER

We have a lot to cover in this step. Now that you've decided that you're committed to the process and purpose of coaching, it's time to turn your purpose into profit. One of the biggest struggles, outside of defining your niché, is knowing how to price your coaching program accordingly. In the previous step, we talked about your call to action and how important it is to conclude every story with the opportunity to work with you. There are so many coaches who stop at telling the story and never ask for the sell. Your offer is what can propel you into six-figures or keep you stuck. All of the internal and mindset work we've worked through over the last eight steps was to build up enough courage to ask for the sale. Refer back to the stronghold that kept me from asking for the sale. I was one of the coaches who would share my story, but not ask for the sale because of rejection. I was afraid that someone would tell me "no" or reject me because they didn't think my program was worth the price I was asking. Your offer is the extended opportunity to work with you either one on one, in a group, or in a pre-recorded program. Most six-figure coaches shy away from one on one coaching and build their multiple six-figure businesses using the group coaching model. I don't encourage you either way; I want you to coach in a space that's most comfortable for you. If you want to coach one on one, then we will have to position your message and market so that it attracts the type of client who will make a higher-end investment. When it comes to making your offer, you have to decide your business model. Will you focus on pushing one high-end offer, or are you looking to offer a variety of opportunities for someone to work with you. I use to offer many different ways to work with me, but it became way too exhausting. I noticed that what I was offering in the lower ticket offer, I was teaching in the higher-end experience. It was making my job harder.

VALUE OVER VOLUME

Before we get too far into pricing, I want to introduce my "value over volume" concept. When I first started coaching, I was sitting in my office, and I asked God to bless me with 8-10 clients per week at $100 per client. That gave me $1000 per week and $4000 per month. I thought this was an ambitious request. It was enough to pay my bills at the time. I thought I was really reaching for the stars, and I'll be honest, God gave me exactly what I had prayed for. I was working three times as hard, and I was exhausted and overworked. On top of a low pay grade, I hadn't yet narrowed my niche. I was coaching every entrepreneur in every area. If you've ever worked with me, you know my experiences are transforming. I thought I needed more clients instead of desiring more income from the client. I didn't know how to price myself where I wouldn't overwork myself and still love what I did. I struggled.

After many years of trial and error, bumping my head against the wall, and wanting to quit, the Holy Spirit began to show me another way. I lived by the idea of "volume over value" (monetary value) for a long time. My goal was to change the masses, and I was okay with coaching 1000 people for $100. My struggle came in when I tried to get 1000 people in one month. I struggled with ten a week. I didn't know what coaching ten clients per week required of me. What I learned in that season is that God had truly given me a gift. Working with entrepreneurs for hours took more out of me than I was prepared to give. I was a wife and mother to three toddlers, and this coaching business was wearing me down. Plus, people around me told me that my business was ministry. They suggested that I appeal to the people who needed my help but couldn't afford to invest the price I had desired. The price that would give me financial freedom for my family. I didn't want to run my own business to make a little more than what I would at a job. I wanted to grow an enterprise and not only pay my salary, but pay my team's salary of six-figures or more. I struggled.

Eventually, my surroundings changed, and the only voice I could hear was God. He told me to refer to His Word that says He gave me the power to gain wealth (Deuteronomy 8:18). He also said that I shall be the lender and not the borrower

(Deuteronomy 28:12). Now how was I supposed to lend when I had nothing to lend? How was I supposed to lend if I still needed to borrow? When it came down to pricing my offer, I struggled. I struggled with assuming what people would invest in and if my program would be worth the investment.

Does any of this sound familiar? Here's what I've concluded, not just for me, but for you as well. People will invest in what they want; it is not our job to figure out how they will do it. With confidence and results come boldness. Money is a mindset, and the moment you shift the way you view money, you will totally shift the way you do pricing. Back in step four, you had to determine whether your coaching business was designed to shift your client's mindset or shift the moment. I decided my coaching business would shift the mindset, and with this decision, I first had to shift my mindset.

We'll get a lot deeper into the mindset shift later in the book. I want to focus on your business model and how you plan to reach your six-figure goal. Will it be by offering a $97 program to 25 clients per month or a $997 program to five clients? The same amount of effort it will require you to get 25 clients will require the same amount of effort to get five, so why not increase the quality of your program and hit your goal? My "Five over 25" rule is what changed my business model forever. I use to work hard looking for 25 clients per month. After changing the way I value my coaching gift and watching the transformation in people's lives right before my eyes, I wanted to spend my time coaching, not looking to enroll 25 clients per month to coach. I'd rather work with the five solid, ideal clients and over-deliver than work with 25 clients and under-deliver. Your price serves as a level of accountability for both you and your client. When you're offering a high-end service, you tend to show up differently—both you and your client. "Value over volume" forces you to show up differently in your business and offer a quality experience for your client. Don't get me wrong, there are coaches who offer low-end programs and show up with great excellence, but they are missing out on a financial breakthrough when they cheat themselves from financial freedom.

PRICE TO PROFIT

When you're building a coaching business with a Christ-centered core, it can seem extremely difficult to price your coaching offer at an investment that will grow your business and sustain your lifestyle. There are usually one of two reasons: either 1) you experience the ministry guilt, believing that because it's for God it has to be free, or 2) you've become comfortable with how your employer values your work, you can't see how Christ values your gifts monetarily. When it comes to pricing your offer, there are two major transformations you're going to have to go through: a mindset transformation and a transformation in your confidence. If one of America's #1 jewelry companies can sell an oversized paperclip for $1,800, then you can sell a program that will transform the lives of your clients and not feel the guilt. Pricing requires you to shift your thinking and your words in three areas:

1. Shift your mindset from "I can't afford" to "I can't afford not to." Affordability is a mindset. The more you assume what people can afford, the longer you'll stay stuck in the vicious cycle of what I consider "pity pricing"—pricing your offer based on someone else's emotions or outlook on affordability. You can afford anything you desire to have. Will it require discipline, a plan, maybe even a little time? Maybe. But saying you can't afford something prevents you from even creating ways to afford it. Affordability is limited based on the mindset of a person.

2. Change your language. There are two ideas that make me cringe when I hear people make these types of confessions aloud: being "broke" and regarding things as "too expensive." You're not "broke," your mindset is. Every service and product has an ideal client; if you think something is too expensive, you are not that manufacturer's ideal client. Don't project your limited thinking onto someone else because you value things differently. Change the way you think, and it'll change the way you live.

3. Invest what you expect to gain. This one right here is a big one. If you want someone to invest $10,000, then you have to be willing to invest $10,000 into someone else's. The law of reciprocity is real, or what I like to teach "sowing and reaping." Galatians 6:7 says, "Be not deceived, God is not mocked, for whatever one sows, that will he also reap." I am a strong believer in backing up the principles

I live by with the Word of God. If you're looking to reach your six-figure goal in your coaching business this year, then it's time to put your money where your faith is. Find a coaching program and invest. This investment is a seed. A seed that is planted on behalf of your business and will reap a harvest. What type of harvest do you expect to receive?

Your coaching business should be designed to bring you purpose, profit, and potential. Here's what I've learned about pricing my program at a four-figure offer: not only will the client show up, but she is expecting to win. Remember back in step six when we talked about the different marketing layers? This is the enrolled client, the type of client who will potentially bring you more clients and have proven results in her business. Your price point is what drives the confidence of your enrolled client. Either she will continue to procrastinate, or she will work her investment. The level of faith in your program and the results your clients can attain shift when the investment is at a certain price point. In the world of entrepreneurship, we're encouraged to research your competitors and price accordingly. You have to decide if you're in business to compete and win or if you're in business to collaborate and change lives. When you price yourself according to your competitors, your focus shifts from helping people to beating your component. This mindset then shifts the intent of the business.

In certain industries, I understand why completing an industry analysis is important, but here in the coaching industry there should be no competition—especially if we're all doing this to serve Christ. Your client is your client. Do you want to stand out in the industry? Of course, but not by manipulation. There is a difference between manipulating your audience into buying by promising them false results just to stay ahead of your competitor and persuading your client to buy so that you can help them change their perspective and life. This is not to be confused with imposter syndrome, which we will discuss later in. Manipulation is control; persuasion is perspective. Build a message that shifts your clients' perspectives. Don't try to control who they will invest in so that you can win.

When selecting your price, also consider your ideal client and the words you use to speak to her. Adjust your pricing according to the type of client you want to show up. Your pricing reflects your words and the type of client you attract. When you have a low price point, you tend to attract a different type of client than you would attract with a high price point. Now I'll be honest: I've had clients enroll into my programs at $100 and $1,000 and give me the same results. I've had clients enroll at $100 and $1,000 and give me completely different results. The right wording plus your pricing will get you closer and closer to the client who will invest, show up, do the work, and get results. I get it; pricing can be a little intimidating. The only way for you to price like an expert and with confidence is to first believe in the transformation you bring and that your strategies are worth the investment.

God has called you to be the bridge. I believe as Christian coaches, we are the bridge between the struggle and the savior. Our strategies are designed to help them get from where they are to where they desire to be. No, I'm not insinuating that your coaching programs should be filled with religion; I'm saying that as a coach, your heart should be filled with relationship. Having the Holy Spirit guide you through coaching sessions is a miraculous experience. Make Christ the CEO of your business; ask Him how to fulfill the vision He's shown you. Seek Him first above all things, and all will be added unto you and your business (Matthew 6:33). When you begin to trust God in your business and the clients He will bring your way, pricing becomes a lot easier. I know the saying, "If it doesn't scare you, then it's not big enough." Well, I don't want you to be afraid because fear is loud. If you're afraid to say it, your potential client will be afraid to invest it. You have to be confident in your price. Our goal is to help take your coaching business from *Start to Six-Figures*, and I teach the coaches in my program how to build and price four-figure programs. At a four-figure investment, we can reach our six-figure goal with no problem.

Here's the math:

Your 4-Figure offer - $1,297

Your annual goal - $108,000

Your quarterly goal is $27,000

Your Monthly goal is $9,000

Your weekly goal is $2,250

Your daily goal is $375

How many clients do you need per month to reach your goal? You will need only eight clients per month to reach your revenue goal.

Imagine what this process will look like as you increase the experience and the investment for the client.

When identifying your price point, be sure that you examine your monthly expenses to ensure you aren't charging less than what you can cover each month in expenses. This was a huge mistake I made in my business. I had a beautiful four-office suite with a fully furnished conference space and reception area. I prayed for this space, and I was so excited to envision all of the plans I had for it. The problem was that I never sat down to count the cost. I had people on payroll, monthly expenses, and I barely saw a take-home income. I assumed this type of struggle was required when first starting a business. I quickly learned that the way I started my multiple six-figure coaching business was all wrong. I was struggling financially because my mindset wasn't in the right place. I was assuming what people could afford and overlooking my value. A piece of my business was a ministry, and I never wanted people to think I was chasing profit. I wanted to be known for chasing purpose, but in the midst of my broken thinking, my family went without. I was more focused on pleasing my clients and my team than building a sustainable business. I'll never forget the year I filed taxes, and my CPA said, "If you keep going at this rate, the IRS will file your business as a hobby." That was the moment I had to decide whether or not I was going to keep playing small or build a business that would create financial freedom, sustainability, and wealth for my family. Price for profit, not pity. As we continue through the 12 steps, we will talk more about scaling your coaching business and how to create a financial nest to pay your team, invest in new programs, and pay yourself.

Step 10

SHIFT YOUR MINDSET

Step 10
SHIFT YOUR MINDSET

*B*e not conformed to this world, but be ye transformed by the renewing of your mind (Romans 12:2). We've explored nine steps of my 12 step six-figure success system, and this step is the most important of them all. When we were children, most of us were told to go to college, get a degree, get married, have children, and live happily ever after. Many of us weren't told to live our best life doing the exact thing Christ died on the cross for us to do. Even if you were told to chase your dreams, there were still limits and restrictions. God sent His Son that we may live and live life more abundantly (John 10:10). The one part of that scripture I want you to take note of is, "The thief cometh not, but to steal, kill and destroy." He's come to destroy anything God has put in you so that you don't live in abundance. The mental assaults are weapons to destroy God's destiny for your life. The coaching industry forces you to break the rules of this world and live the life Christ anticipated for you to live. The sky is the limit. This industry completely disrupts what many of us were raised to accomplish in our lives. I've seen coaches price their programs from $100 to $100,000. You can become whatever you desire as long as you believe that, with God, all things are possible. Your mindset is your most powerful weapon; it can build you up or destroy you. It's the first voice you hear when you wake up and the last one before you go to bed. Will you allow this voice to keep you stuck, or will you remove the limits and go after everything you deserve?

FIGHTING THE MENTAL ASSAULTS

As I've grown my coaching business, I've experienced some highs and lows. I've experienced the tears of wanting to give up and the thoughts of never making it. I host an annual anthology for the coaches inside of my program, and in the second volume my chapter is called "Diary of a Depressed Entrepreneur." During that season of my life and business, I had experienced so many mental assaults. I couldn't bear it. I was about ready to throw in the towel. I didn't know what was going on. My thoughts were trying to rip me apart. I knew depression was generational in my family, but I couldn't understand why I felt the way I did. If I don't believe anything in the world, I believe in the Word of God. I know that once His principles are applied, life changes. The enemy was after my destiny, but God was showing me the exact experiences that my ideal clients may go through. The assault of limiting beliefs, imposter syndrome, and self-sabotaging thoughts and behaviors.

Limiting Beliefs—having a hard time believing that you really can. I challenge you to find the root of this deceitful thought. Where did it start? How did it mature? Get to the heart of why you have a hard time believing you can. One reason I struggled, and sometimes still do, is because I've never seen anyone I knew reach six-figures in her coaching business. I've seen people on the internet and heard a few stories, but I've never personally seen someone take a business—let alone a coaching business—from scratch to six-figure success. I knew that if I went to college, received a degree, and worked at a job for a few years, I could break the poverty line. I never imagined I could start my own business doing the exact thing I love and make multiple six-figures monthly. In the world I was raised in, making that type of money was never a possibility. It's time to remove the limiting beliefs and reach for what once seemed impossible.

Examine your thoughts: there should never be a time you joke about the success of your business or the value you offer in the lives of others. Examine areas in your life where you found yourself speaking negatively about yourself and your business. Can you recall those thoughts? Write them down. Once you've identified the times you've spoken against the growth of your business, write a statement renouncing that thought and find scripture that confirms it.

Example

Old thought: I'll never earn six-figures in my coaching business.

New thought: I am a six-figure earner in my coaching business. According to Deuteronomy 8:18, I have the power to gain wealth.

Examine your behavior: what behaviors do you have in your business that could be magnifying your limiting beliefs. How often do you work on your business? How many times have you given a "family discount"? When was the last time you invested? What do you allow others to say about your business? How do you allow people to treat your gift and your time? We think limiting beliefs will only show up in our thoughts, but if you're thinking it, most likely, there is a behavior following it. Have you structured your coaching business as an actual business? Filing taxes, completing your limited liability company filing within your state, written out your SOP's? Federally trademarking your name? The way you treat your business is how others will treat your business. Change how you do business and show up as the expert.

Examine your beliefs: What do you really believe about yourself and your business? If you're struggling with self-confidence, then most likely, you'll struggle with showing up as the expert in your coaching business. If you don't believe that you're beautiful, amazing, and smart, then you will struggle with pricing your coaching offers like a six-figure expert. What do you really believe? What you believe is what you will accomplish. Remember, every thought is a seed that is sown by your words. Change what you think is possible.

When these types of thoughts begin to surface and attempt to talk you out of your destiny, the only way to defeat them is to face them. Check them and speak life about yourself and your business out loud against them. Your words have power; negative talk will only dig a deeper hole. Use your words to build yourself up. Remind yourself of how amazing you truly are and how God placed you in this industry to change and impact lives.

IMPOSTER SYNDROME

With the type of program I offer, I struggled big-time in this area. I didn't even know this was a thing. I struggled with feeling inadequate, like I wasn't qualified to teach what I teach. This was an internal battle I struggled with for a long time. If you were to ask how I got over imposter syndrome, I would say through knowing who God is in my life and in my business. There were times I would read a book for the first time, and it would teach the exact things I've taught in my trainings. That, for me, was evidence of the gift God had given me. Not only did I begin to shift the focus from what *I* was able to do to what *God* was doing through me, I practiced. I put my strategies out there anyway, and time after time, sometimes I would hit a wall, but most times I would get amazing results. Notice the signs; when you see something that confirms your gift in coaching, don't brush it off. Stop, recognize it, and then show gratitude. This is what built my confidence and showed me that what I do isn't fraudulent. There is actual transformation taking place in the lives of those God has empowered me to serve and impact.

Examine your thoughts: Are your thoughts telling you that what you're doing isn't worth a four-figure investment? Are your thoughts telling you that you're stealing people's money and you're a con just like the rest of the world? These types of thoughts are driven by the enemy to keep you from believing in yourself and fulfilling God's purpose for your life. As you grow in your coaching business, this type of thinking may show up periodically, but you have to learn how to speak against those thoughts and press toward the vision God has shown you. Take a moment and identify a time you've had this type of experience—when you felt like no one should pay you for service.

Example:

Old thought: I can't charge $1,297 for this; I can't see how it's worth it.

New thought: My starting rate is $1,297, and I know I help my clients gain transformational results. According to 1 John 4:9, God sent His only begotten Son into the world, that we might live through Him.

Examine your Behavior: What behaviors do you present that are caused by imposter syndrome? Maybe you're holding back on sharing strategies and information you know, in the pit of your belly, could change lives, but your thoughts are telling you that you're not qualified since you don't have years of academic education. Maybe you're holding back in your coaching sessions or not launching a program. What about your pricing? Have you not increased your prices because you don't feel qualified? Take a moment to examine whether or not imposter syndrome is showing up in your life. Sometimes it can be subtle; you won't even start your coaching business because your thoughts have told you how you're not qualified.

Examine your beliefs: What has imposter syndrome caused you to believe about yourself and your business? Has it forced you to believe that it is impossible for you to reach six-figures in your coaching business? Do you battle with believing you're qualified to serve and support your ideal client in the areas we've identified in previous steps? Remember, your qualifications aren't determined by what someone says; you're qualified because of your experiences and tenacity to heal in your once broken areas through Christ Jesus. No one can tell you what your experiences are worth sharing in the lives of others.

When you start to feel like what you're offering the world is fraudulent, check the root. Why are you feeling this way? What caused the thought? Could it be possible that you're feeling this way because the exact thing your thoughts are trying to prevent you from sharing is the exact thing that will help your ideal client reach where they desire to be in life?

Self-Sabotaging Behaviors: Most of the behaviors I've listed are self-sabotaging behaviors. They are thought patterns and behaviors that hold you back and prevent you from doing what you desire to do in business and in life. This type of behavior is paralyzing. Review the list below of different ways self-sabotaging behaviors show up:

1. Overthinking
2. Lack of commitment and or consistency
3. Consuming content and not implementing it
4. Wanting to be in control of the outcome

Why do we experience self-sabotaging behaviors? In most cases, it's due to a lack of self-value and confidence. An effect of lack of confidence is having a hard time speaking up for yourself and expressing with confidence what you believe. You're afraid of success or failure, and you're not sure how to move forward.

There are three major types of self-sabotaging behaviors:

1. Procrastination
2. Perfectionism
3. Negative Self-Talk

Which one of the three self-sabotaging behaviors do you find yourself falling victim to? Take a moment and examine the self-sabotaging behaviors and beliefs that stop you from reaching your goals in your coaching business. You have the opportunity to become everything you desire in the coaching industry; what thoughts are telling you that you can't? Let's get to the root of your thinking and replace the thoughts that are keeping you stuck with words that will push you forward. Find scripture as your evidence that you, too, can accomplish everything you desire. What does a life of freedom look like to you? How can you live this life and do the exact thing you love?

CHANGE THE MINDSET VS. THE MOMENT

You've heard me mention a few times in this book to check the intentions behind your desire to grow a six-figure coaching business in your niché. Are you coaching to change the moment of your client or the mindset? When you only focus on shifting the moment, you're doing your client a disservice. You're not allowing your client to reach their greatest potential in the area you are called to support them in. When I refer to only shifting the moment, I'm referring to strategies that are temporary, surface-type application. Help your client understand the benefits of changing their perspective. When you shift their perspective, you shift their mindset. When you're only interested in a temporary fix, then the band-aide will only last for a moment, leaving the client untrusting of the next potential solution. Shifting the mindset of your client will last a lifetime. With this type of business model, you must be open and willing to apply personal adjustments so that you deliver an authentic experience. Your mindset shift is not about you. It's about the people you are called to support and serve in your coaching business. It's about being the example that "change" changes lives. Find purpose in your coaching, and profit will follow, but that doesn't mean purpose is free or discounted. Purpose is in the process, not in the price for the process. The price is what holds both you and the client accountable and encourages results and transformation.

WEALTH CREATOR VS. WEALTH GENERATOR

Are you a wealth creator or a wealth generator? Being a wealth creator takes a certain level of tenacity and faith to break free from the limiting beliefs and strongholds that attack a wealth creator. As previously mentioned, wealth generators can take a proven concept and multiply the profit over and over. A wealth creator is someone who has taken an idea, built a business from scratch, and created wealth from it. In the next step, we will talk about scaling and the importance of a wealth generator for your business, but for now, I want to help you recognize the immaculate gift of procreation that lives in your imagination. One of my favorite Bible verses (I'm starting to see that I have many of them) is when God changed Jacob's name to Israel in the book of Genesis. God told him to "be fruitful and multiply, a nation and a company of nations shall be of thee, and kings shall come out of thy loins" (Genesis 35:11). The phrase "be fruitful and multiply" can be found several times throughout the book of Genesis. God not only told the creatures of the sea to be fruitful and multiply, but He also told man and woman (Genesis 1:21-28). Each time the phrase was used, He instructed them to "become many."

When we read this passage, we immediately equate this phrase to having multiple children. However, in chapter 35 verse 11, God instructed Israel, formally known as Jacob, to go out and become many, to increase and bring abundance. He said a multiple of nations, an assembly of people (a company), shall be yours. He said, "and kings shall be birthed from your loins, leaders shall come from your seat of strength (International Standards Bible Encyclopedia, Blueletterbible.org). God wants us to be fruitful and multiply businesses, wealth, and employment. He wants us to operate in His image and create the vision He's planted in our imagination.

If you're reading this book, He's called you to be a wealth creator. Far before conception, He has a plan for you. Plans to prosper and not harm you (Jeremiah 29:11). It is His plan that you create wealth for your family and the generations after you (Deuteronomy 8:18). It is His plan that you teach good tidings unto the suffering, oppressed, and afflicted (Isaiah 61:1). Being a wealth creator is your birthright. Build your business and hire wealth generators. God has given you the vision, write it down, make it plain so that the wealth generators can take it and implement it (Habakkuk 2:2-3). Fear and procrastination will only keep you as a wealth generator for someone else's dream, but taking authority in your rightful place in the world will shift your position from a generator to a creator. Have faith in what God has given you to create wealth and know that, with Him, all things are possible (Mark 10:27).

MONEY ISN'T THE ISSUE

As we've journeyed through the 12 steps, we've focused a lot on your value and how you must adjust the way you see yourself. The growth of your coaching business isn't based on how many likes, shares, or comments you receive, but your mindset and what you believe to be true. It's based on your decision to wake up and say "yes" every day, even when you don't want to or everything around you is telling you not to. The growth of your coaching business isn't decided based on the amount of money you make, but how you view money and the amount that you invest and receive. Money is not your issue; it's the way you think about money. Money is a seed planted in expectation to reap a harvest.. Whether you pay for a house or a coaching program, your money is a seed planted in expectation to reap. Money is an asset to be traded for something of personal value or interest. How do you view $1000? This is a mindset question I ask the coaches in my program. Do you see $1000 as too expensive or as a seed? Do you see it as a lot of money or a valuable exchange? Take a moment and examine how you view money. What's the root of your money mindset? Your money mindset is the root of your potential to earn six-figures in your coaching business. Set your prices according to your offer, not your fear. I want you to consider what it costs to run a six-figure coaching business, sit down and count the cost. What subscriptions do you have coming out each month, have you set aside a budget to hire a coach? What percentage are you setting aside for taxes and business capital? Who will you need to bring onto your team to ensure you're delivering efficiently. These are just a few things you want to consider when you're establishing your price. Don't be so concerned about what people can afford, the question is: at your current rates, can you afford to scale and grow your business? The confidence behind your offer is what will inspire your ideal client to show up with confidence.

In volume three of the *Coach my Life* Anthology, I shared five proven strategies that will shift your thinking into abundance and reveal that money really does grow on trees. For your free copy of "Money Really Does Grow on Trees" email me at money-tree@starttosixfigures.com. Use the diagram in your workbook and attach your vision to a seed. What are you expecting to gain once you plant the seed? Every seed will reap a harvest, no matter the amount. Don't get wrapped up in the amount of the seed, just be obedient. Whatever God tells you sow or invest, be sure to do so. It's not the monetary value of the seed that reaps the harvest, it's your belief that the seed will yield a harvest. The bigger the seed, the bigger your faith (Genesis 26:12). Whether you're sowing into ministry or a coaching program, make it clear of your expectations. Practice this exercise each time you invest into your business. This will help you change how you view money, and it will challenge you to stretch your expectations. Sometimes your initial expectation is not what you receive; your harvest may show up differently. However, if you're prepared to harvest in more than one way, it increases your faith and desire to water and nurture the seed. Access your bonus read "Money Really Does Grow on Trees" for strategies on how to water and nurture your seed. Once you've listed the amount of your seed, be sure to find and list scripture to support your seed. Using the diagram, list your investment or seed amount, scripture, and what you expect to harvest from the seed.

From Start to Six Figures

$_____   Scripture:_____

Step 11

SCALE TO SIX FIGURES

Step 11
SCALE TO SIX FIGURES

How to scale your business from start to six-figures in your niché

Scaling your coaching business takes laser vision. It requires a concrete plan to sustain, grow, and monetize the vision for your business. Scaling your coaching business can give you the freedom to create generational wealth for you and those you bring to your team to help bring forth the vision. It creates the opportunity to generate income in your business at a much quicker pace while offering quality services and transformational experiences to your clients. Throughout this chapter, we will address each focus area of scaling your coaching business and how to implement each area without overwhelming your process and becoming discouraged.

Count the Cost – What will it take for you to scale your business? This focus area will require you to examine the cost of scaling your coaching business. Who do you need to hire? What software will you need to purchase so that your team and clients are working efficiently? What software will you use for your client onboarding, scheduling, and payments? Take a moment and write out the plan. You want to be clear of what you will need to run your coaching business with precise efficiency using automation and a team. What's your operating budget? How much do you need in the bank to ensure that payroll, taxes, and operating expenses are being covered (Luke 14:28)?

One of the best lessons I've learned is having multiple bank accounts to allocate funds for the appropriate time. To start, you should have three bank accounts. The first account is to set aside taxes. For a six-figure year, you should be setting aside, at minimum, $3,000 a quarter. This business strategy will keep you out of financial trouble in the long run. Your second account should be capital so that your business is never broke (and not a broken mindset, but broke like no money). It's really hard to run a business from client to client. In the 9-5 world, we run from living paycheck to paycheck, but nothing is worse than living client to client. This is why your price points must be at a specific number. It helps eliminate stressful months when the business enrollment numbers may be down. Divide your income. How much will go into each account? Your third account is your cashflow account. This is where your team, including yourself, is compensated, and you're reinvesting into your business—whether it be hiring a coach, enrolling into a program, or paying for advertisement. If the goal is $9000 per month, then we can divide your monthly income as follows:

Account #1 - $1,000

Account #2 - $2,000

Account #3 - $6,000

Now, keep in mind this is just an example. Maybe you want to use account #2 to invest in a coach after you've saved a little. There is no right or wrong way to divide your income if you're setting aside enough to run your business. You also want to look at your personal expenses and be sure you're able to pay yourself and the contractors you bring in when needed. If you need to bring team members on a per-project basis or part-time, it's ok. You don't want to exhaust your monthly budget.

Decide the Model – When you start thinking about scaling your business, the easiest way to create a money-making machine is to identify which business model works best for your business and work it until it's producing clients consistently. Which business model works well with your style of coaching?

One-on-One Coaching – Using this model may be a little more difficult to scale than others, unless you have a team of coaches who you are assigning clients to. This model is definitely possible, but it requires more capital to sustain.

Group Coaching – This is the most common model used to scale in the coaching industry. You're able to offer your signature solution to anywhere from two to 200 people at a particular price point and vastly increase your annual profits.

Hybrid Coaching – This is my favorite business model. It's the model we use in the Chase Great Niche Certification Program where you're able to access both one-on-one and group coaching in one program.

Programs and Courses (evergreen)– this model offers a "hands-off approach." You can host programs live during a specific time of the year, or you can pre-record content and make the program available to your client. You can also combine this with hybrid coaching and offer courses and coaching. I've found this to be more efficient for my coaching program.

Membership Site – while most membership sites offer a low monthly enrollment, they can be used to scale your business. This model will reflect the volume over value model, but it is doable.

Corporate – this model only allows you to work with corporate clients.

I was the coach who tried to offer multiple programs to try and appeal to different clients in my target audience. It had become exhausting and overwhelming. Not only did it feel like I was always trying to get someone to sign up for my latest program, but I noticed that all of my smaller programs were offering similar content as my bigger program, and I was cutting myself short. Once I decided to focus on pushing one program, it made my monthly marketing and content a lot easier to manage and reproduce. This model also gives me a better projection of my monthly financial goals. Now, instead of offering several small programs and the option to work with me one-on-one, I offer my annual in-person event for Christian female startup coaches and my premium program that includes all of the content of my smaller programs plus more.

Master the Message – with deciding your business model, you want to have a simple, specific, and clear message to your audience. The clearer your message and your model become, the more you will attract clients who are ready to invest and learn. When scaling, don't overcomplicate the message. Create a direct road to buy. When your client is clear on the exact problem you're going to help them solve and the program that will solve it, it makes it easier for them to press "buy." I believe offering one program that solves one problem is a sure-fire way to reach six-figures within 12 months. The more laser-focused your marketing message becomes, the more your program is magnified before your ideal client. This isn't to say that you don't or can't have other content and programs to offer, but you need to make sure that there is one way to get into your funnel. Afterward, you can upsell and offer other programs and opportunities to work with you. When your marketing is simple and specific, it makes it easier for the client to decide. When you give clients too many options, in most cases, it overwhelms them and leaves them without a solution and you without clients.

Identify Your Process – Map out your process. This is where your standard operating procedures (SOP) will come in handy. Don't be like me, bringing new people to the team and not having a standard process of how the system should flow. There are two ways you can go about this process: you can bring on a new person and build out the SOP's together, or you take the time to build them out before hire. Either way, this is an extremely important step to scaling. Identify the first five steps of your process and write out the procedure.

Lead Generation – How are you producing new leads? How are you keeping up with warm and cold leads? Have you invested in a CRM (Customer Relationship Manager)? Is this process clear and in detail?

Client Onboarding – How will you onboard your new clients? This should be an automated experience. Once your client presses buy, there should be an email sequence of what your client should do next.

Automations – What emails need to be sent to your new or existing clients? What do you need to put on an automation system?

Client Journey – what does your client journey look like? From the time they enroll until they are complete with your program?

Client Offboard – Once your client has completed your program, what's next? Do you transition them into a community, offer them an upsell, or ask for referrals and testimonials?

Pricing – What is your price for your program? Do you offer payment plans, if so, how long is the payment plan? Make sure to revisit section #1 of this chapter when determining your price.

Count the cost. After reviewing your expenses, including payroll, how much is your program? This is the best part of creating processes for your company. Once you've identified a price, stick with it. This type of decision-making establishes integrity and trust in your business. Due to the nature of this book, I encourage you to price your program at four-figures or more. This will help you reach your six-figure goal and encourage you to deliver quality content and a transformational experience.

Package – How will you deliver your content to your client? Keep in mind, the way you deliver is based on the business model you've selected in section #2 of this chapter. If you're offering programs and courses, select a platform that is user-friendly for the client and offers email automation. If you're offering group or one-on-one coaching, how does this process look? How will they schedule their one-on-one calls or join the group sessions? Make this process as user-friendly as possible. Scaling your coaching business is incorporating systems and processes that will increase your monthly profit through automation. Figuring out how you will deliver your content may take trial and error. You may not need to change your business system; just adjust how you deliver the content.

Sales Funnel – This is not as complicated as the industry gurus make it out to be. When we talk about funnels, we're talking about the pathway from potential client to paid client. I've seen sales funnels with up to 8 layers between the initial contact and the actual sale. Now, I'll be honest; my system is not that complicated. In most instances, you will get 1-2 layers before we ask for the sale. Review the different ways you can get your client to book a call or into your sales funnel.

Masterclass – a free training that offers your client a small win that is concluded by a call to action

Facebook Ad – this most times leads to a free offer, either a masterclass, challenge, or Facebook group. You can set up an ad for a paid program, but I've always found it to be a little more difficult to sell a high offer through an ad. Now, this is not to say that it isn't possible. I've just seen better results offering a freebie that will get them into my email community where I can nurture the relationship, offer more valuable content, and then position a call to action for a high-end offer.

Lead Magnet – this is content you offer your potential client in exchange for their email address. This is free content that can be in the form of a vlog, masterclass, or pdf. Be creative. The more attractive your lead magnet, the more potential clients you can get onto your email list.

Email Marketing – this is a long-term nurturing opportunity that will definitely help bring in new clients. Your email sequence provides the opportunity to educate your client on how you can support them in their transformation. Make sure to have a powerful subject line for open conversion, then the rest is up to you and how you educate and connect in the body of your email. This process may take a little longer, but slow drips will still fill a pale.

As I've shared throughout this book, coaching is not cookie cutter. The way you set up your sales funnel is completely up to you. I don't need to click eight times before I decide to buy, and so far, neither does my ideal client; however, each company is different. Build your coaching using strategies that will compliment your personality and reach your revenue goals.

Hire a Team – write the vision and make it plain so that those who read it can take it and run (Habakkuk 2:2-3). Before building your team, revisit your plan in section #1 "Count the Cost." Map out the position of every person who will help take the vision to the next level. When you think of hiring, ask yourself, "Who can I bring onto the team to multiply my time, scale my time, and make money on my time?" This is how I decided to hire my first three employees. Not only do you want to hire wisely, but you want to be clear about how they can support the vision of your company. Review your monthly budget for payroll. Who can you bring in part-time or on a per-project basis? Don't exhaust yourself thinking you need to hire multiple people when you're not bringing in the income to cover their cost. You shouldn't have to take personal income to fund payroll. Use the money you're making in your business and cover your expenses. If you're not making the money yet, then it may not be time to hire. I often hear about coaches hiring team members, but they have yet to consistently generate clients to cover the cost. You don't need a virtual assistant (VA) to manage your emails when your email traffic is manageable. Conversely, don't wait until the last minute to hire because then you're looking for someone to rescue you instead of build with you.

Create a timeline in your business and decide which financial goals you will accomplish before you hire a new team member. Hiring team members and outsourcing work is not the same thing. If you're not good at graphic design, then, yes, outsource that task. But there are some elements of your business I encourage you to learn. Sales pages, landing pages, email marketing... while these may not be fun, establish a voice for your company before you bring in someone to create one for you. Write out every position, the description, and the number of hours required to complete the tasks you will be delegating. Then write out a budget; how much can you pay each person? Determine this budget based on a growth scale. Don't come out with a high investment if it'll strip the company of cashflow. If all you can contribute is $500 a month, then find someone who can bring quality work at the rate you have available.

What do you need to successfully scale your business? What practices and policies can you implement now so that you're starting off as a six-figure business? If you're just getting started or you've been practicing for a while, establish a foundation. What days will you work on the business, and what days will you work in the business? Working on the business consists of content development, infrastructure, and projects. Working in the business consists of working with clients, coaching, sales calls, trainings, etc. Create a routine in your business and map out time to fulfill every position you intend to hire for. Outsource when you begin to spend too much time in an area or if your DIY isn't producing the results you desire. Think beyond your surroundings. Find a company that is already operating the way you desire for inspiration. If they can do it, so can you.

Step 12

START TO SIX FIGURES

Step 12
START TO SIX FIGURES

I've shared a lot of content over the last 12 steps, but this isn't everything. This is just enough to get you started and focused. I encourage you to take this process one step at a time and don't overthink it. Don't spend so much time trying to perfect the message that you never put it out to the world to see if it's a good fit. This is my 12 step process. This is the process the Holy Spirit allowed me to journey through so that I can stand before you and tell you that even during the weary days and crying nights, it can happen for you. Don't let the world make you think that your dreams are impossible; God would have never allowed you to imagine them if they were impossible. I like to look at our imagination like a movie cinema, showing us bite-size pieces of what's possible if we continue to believe and implement.

Just a quick review of all 12 steps:

1. Accept the challenge; it'll change someone's life.
2. Submit to the process; it's where you'll build character and receive clarity.
3. Decide there is no other option; this will help eliminate your plan B.
4. Master your message; it's your vehicle to six-figures.
5. Solve a problem; it's your credibility as an expert.
6. Why Niché Marketing for Christian coaches? Because it will help you stand out in the industry.
7. Know your ideal client; it's who you once were.
8. Tell the story, don't sell your service. We all have similar services, but our stories are what make us different.
9. Make an offer and ask for the sale; it's business.
10. Shift your mindset and break free from what you think is impossible.
11. Scale to six-figures and create financial sustainability for your family.
12. From *Start to Six-Figures* is a process, but you can accomplish it as long as you stay consistent and committed.

START

Start your coaching business with the intention to scale not just to sell. This was one of my first of many mistakes when I started my coaching business. Because of my lack of knowledge, I didn't start a six-figure coaching business, I started a business and wanted to coach. Take the time to write the vision and become clear of your expectations in the company. Are you coaching as a hobby, or is your goal to one day transition from a dual-preneur to a full-time business owner? Who will be affected by the growth of your business, and how will it affect them? Think about the type of example you're setting and the generational curses you're breaking. When you first entered into the coaching industry, what did you envision? What did you see? Go back to that place and stay focused. If the goal is to create an evergreen coaching program that runs off automation, then build out the program and commit to the process. As Christian female startup coaches, we aren't in the industry to solve the most popular problem; we're in the industry to the problem God assigned us to solve. Don't get distracted by the noise. The world will tell you to find a niché that is attractive to people; I encourage you to discover the niché that pleases God and fulfills purpose. There is a much greater reward. If you've been hesitant about starting or increasing your prices, this is the moment I want you to decide your next move. Will you grow, or will you stay stuck?

From Start to Six Figures

How to Start your Six-Figure Coaching Business?

1. Start as the expert, not as an experiment. This is not a trial run, don't fake it until you make it; do the work. Get clarity on your message and the problem you solve.

2. Price with confidence. You have the power to determine what's considered a low offer. To some people, a $997 investment is a low price point. Don't be fooled into thinking you have to start small. The world doesn't need to know you're new. Being new is not a reason; it's an excuse. It's not a reason to price low; it's what you tell yourself to justify your fear of asking for what you truly desire.

3. Narrow your niché and magnify your message.

To access this live training, visit coachlatoya.com/connect

SIX FIGURES

To some, six-figures may be a big deal. To some, it may only be the beginning, but here, it's a start. Give yourself room to want more and be okay with it. Six-figures only seems big to the person who doesn't believe she can achieve it; it'll then seem small to the person who's surpassed it. On which side of the fence do you prefer to be? You started a business to make money and transform lives. Don't get so consumed in the transformation that you don't make money, and don't get so consumed in making money that you lose the transformation. What can you do with six-figures in your coaching business this year? See it, believe it, and write it out. Review my Six-Figure Cycle below and fit your business into this cycle.

Ministry: How does your coaching align with the Word of God?

Message: What is your crystal-clear message?

Mindset: Do your thoughts stop you or catapult you into six-figures?

Mindy: Mindy is my ideal client. Who is your ideal client, and how does your ideal client remind you of yourself? Identify the behaviors and beliefs.

Market: How will you use your message to speak to Mindy in your copy?

Monetize: How will you monetize and scale your six-figure coaching business?

Mindset: What's your daily confession? What scripture will you reference as evidence that you really can win.

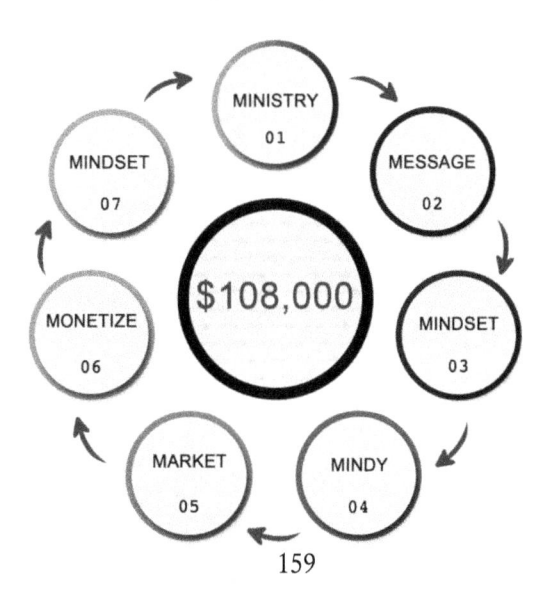

CONGRATULATIONS

*Y*ou have successfully completed my 12 Step Six-Figure Success System, and I am so happy to have been a part of your journey. I pray that during this book, you received the exact steps needed to change your hobby to a full-time business and go after the exact thing God has called you to do. Trust me, this journey isn't for the weak, but that's ok because He's called you to it, His strongest. You've got this!

If you're looking for community and support, be sure to download the workbook as an additional resource and join our on-demand content and coaching community.

To join the Niche Certification Program for Christian Female Startup Coaches and take your coaching business from *Start to Six-Figures* in your niché, visit coachlatoya.com/call and schedule your enrollment call today!

To access my free tool, "How to Start a Six-Figure Coaching Business," visit coachlatoya.com/connect.

Prayer for the Six-Figure Coach

Father God, in the name of your son Jesus Christ, I come to you in agreement with my sister who is reading this book that this year, with faith and work, she will reach six-figures in her coaching business. Lord, I thank you for her; I thank you for the dreams that you've placed before her. I thank you for choosing her to be a vessel for your Word, to deliver it to your people in the form of coaching. Lord, your Word says whatever we bind on earth, you'll bind in heaven. Lord, I bind up every attack of the enemy that will come against my sister's thoughts, confidence, and ability to believe bigger in her business. Lord, I loose confidence, vision, and clarity.

Lord, I thank you for my sister; I thank you for the clients you are sending to her in this very moment. I thank you for the team you are building for her right before her eyes. Lord, I thank you for giving her a little more patience to endure the process and a lot more courage to go after everything she desires in the process.

Lord, I ask that you cover her support system: her children, husband, family, and friends. Whoever is contributing to her journey, Lord, I ask that you bless them in Jesus' name. Now Lord, I ask that this book not be where she ends, but where she begins. I ask that this book ignites a fire in her belly that eliminates every thought of doubt and fear that once kept her from believing in what you can truly do in her life. Lord, I pray for clients—that every person who enrolls into her program shall be blessed and transformed in Jesus' name. Clients will refer clients; friends will refer friends, and every person she works with will value her value and invest in her gift. Lord, I come against sickness and diseases, mental assaults, depression, and fear right now in the name Jesus. Your daughter will walk in the authority that you have established for us. Lord, I pray that every seed she sows, reaps a harvest. In the matchless name of our Lord and Savior Jesus Christ, we pray. Amen.

Xoxo,

Your Vision Coach,

LaToya Early

Acknowlegements

I am so grateful for my team, for being patient with me during this writing process. I appreciate the creative feedback and encouragement when I wanted to procrastinate.

I am grateful for my husband, A Dad Coach, for stepping up with the house and kids and allowing me to finish this project on such a strict timeline. I wouldn't be who I am if it weren't for the team I have at home.

To my Dads, I did it! #missingmydads

About the Author
LATOYA EARLY

LaToya is a wife, woman of God, mother of three amazing young men, Vision Coach, Empowerment Trainer, six-time author, and founder of Chase Great Enterprises. LaToya has creatively organized a community of coaches where she helps Christian Female Startup Coaches start, grow, and monetize their coaching business from Start to six-figures in their niche.

While working in her company full-time, LaToya has published several personal development books and organized three volumes of the Coach My Life anthology. She has been honored by her home city, Detroit, Michigan, with the Spirit of Detroit award, received entrepreneur of the year, and has been recognized by business and organizations for her ability to help coaches and entrepreneurs dig deep and build businesses that solve problems. She has been featured on an array of inspirational women blogs, television, radio, and podcast shows; she has keynoted conferences, women empowerment events, and commencement ceremonies.

LaToya is focused on helping 1000 coaches start, grow, and monetize their coaching business from start to six-figures over the next 12 months.

If you're ready to start, grow and monetize your coaching business and become certified in your niche' lets connect.

Visit visit **www.chasegreatenterprises.com** for your free masterclass on how to start your coaching business.

Become the Expert in your Coaching Niche'.

- Discover Your Niche'
- Master Your Message
- Monetize Your Programs

Complete program in 6 months or less!

NICHE CERTIFIED
CHASE GREAT

Share your success on social media using #coachmylife

Coach My Life®

Anthology Series

Now available at www.CoachMyLife.com.

CPSIA information can be obtained
at www.ICGtesting.com
Printed in the USA
JSHW031950070521
14497JS00005B/9